W9-CMZ-120

Profiles from History

Stories of Those Who Are Worthy of Remembrance

- Volume 1 -

Ashley M. Wiggers

Profiles from History - Volume 1
Copyright © 2009, 2011, 2012, 2015 Ashley M. Wiggers, Geography Matters

Portrait Illustrations © 2009 Cheryl Ellicott
Map Illustrations by Kathy Wright

All rights reserved. Activity pages, reports, maps, and flags may be photocopied by
the original purchaser for personal and household use only. Such reproductions
may not be sold or given away. Except for the limited authorization to photocopy
stated above, no part of this book may be reproduced or transmitted in any form
or by any means, electronic or mechanical, including photocopying, recording,
or by any information storage and retrieval system, without permission from the
publisher in writing.

ISBN: 978-1-931397-57-5
Library of Congress Control Number: 2009902868

Published by Geography Matters, Inc.
800.426.4650
www.geomatters.com

Printed in the United States of America

Dedication

To all those I love, thank you for your encouragement and support.

My husband, thank you for your incredible love and friendship. You inspire my every creativity. My parents, thank you for teaching me how to write, and always telling me I could do anything. Linda, my editor and dear friend, thank you for your patience and wisdom.

And my heavenly father to whom I owe all the glory, and praise.

Table of Contents

Instructions

The greatest connection we can have throughout history is the human one. I tried to take a unique perspective on each historical figure by sharing some of the lesser-known facts that you may not have learned before. For instance, instead of focusing on Benjamin Franklin's many inventions, I focused more on his strength of character. As you read each profile it is my hope that you will connect with the person, not just the history.

In this book you will read about inventors, artists, statesmen, and explorers that made a significant difference in the world around them and forever changed the future. Beginning in the year 1200 and continuing through 1890, the exploits of many famous people are described with an eye to seeing their motivations and the impact their lives had on others.

Use *Profiles from History* either to enhance lessons in history and social studies or as a stand-alone book. Choose the fun projects in this book according to the interests of each student. Select as many or as few of the activities as you would like. Each profile can be used as a read-aloud, or your student can use the story for independent reading. To get the full benefit from each profile I recommend students use several of the following activities provided to tap into the different approaches taken:

Discussion questions: inspire critical thinking, and help the student relate to each historical figure.

Follow-up activities: relate to the accomplishments of each profile, connecting the child tactically to the importance of each person's story.

Word games: such as word searches, crossword puzzles, and cloze activities focus on key words to remember from the profile while increasing comprehension and vocabulary.

Critical thinking activities: include sequencing of events and determining true and false statements relating to the story.

Maps: help students visually pinpoint either the location where the historical figure came from, or the area in which the main event of their life took place.

Timelines: give the student an overview of the time period in which the historical figure lived and connect each person with other important events occurring at the same time. A reference timeline is included with each profile. Students are instructed to place timeline figures on a timeline. This timeline and the figures are located in the back of the book before the answer keys.

Also Available

Profiles from History - Volume 1 activities and reproducibles in digital format for your convenience.

If you enjoy the format and focus of this book you may also be interested in:

Profiles from History - Volume 2 which mainly focuses on the heroes of American history during the Revolutionary and Civil Wars.

Profiles from History - Volume 3 highlights those who solved problems and inspired determination, in America and around the world, during our most trying hours.

Marco Polo

From the very beginning, Marco Polo was meant to be an explorer. His father and uncle made long journeys to faraway lands. These trips often kept them away from home for many years at a time. During one such journey Marco's mother died, and when his father finally returned, Marco was ready to join him in the family business. And so he left on his first journey when he was only 17.

While most young men at that time had responsibilities at home, Marco's life was filled with adventure. The Polos' travels took them through many countries in Europe and Asia. They started their trips in Italy and ended up in China, which was called Cathay at the time. The older Polos visited China's great leader, Kublai Khan, while they were there.

Kublai Khan took a liking to the Polo brothers when they first met. The brothers were given a golden tablet, which insured that they would be treated well wherever they traveled in China. Kublai Khan was a powerful leader of a rich and successful country. The cities of Cathay had many modern features such as canals that connected the cities, an elaborate system of messengers similar to the Pony Express, paper money, books and fancy clothes and dishes. There were many interesting and unusual things to see.

As a matter of fact, Marco's life was filled with seeing new things. He stayed in China for 17 years doing various jobs for Kublai Khan. Everywhere he went, he watched the people carefully and tried to learn as much as he could about them and their language, families, and how they lived and worked. When he left China to return home, he remembered all the people, places, and things he had seen.

After his return to Italy, something happened that would change the world. Marco was the captain of a ship involved in a war. He was captured and put into prison. Another man in the prison was a writer and heard Marco's stories. He encouraged Marco to tell him all about his travels so he could write them down. This became the famous book, *The Travels of Marco Polo.*

Even though many people who read Marco's book were not sure that all his adventures were true, the stories were full of new and exciting things and told of fantastic adventures. The book also included descriptions of the places Marco had been, which helped mapmakers make new maps.

To the people who did not travel far from home, Marco's book was like going on an adventure themselves. To those who longed to travel, it gave life to their dreams of visiting faraway places. One such reader was Christopher Columbus. With his love of travel and exploring, it is not hard to imagine how inspiring this book must have been.

Polo himself was inspired. He believed that it was God's will for him to return from China and tell others what he had seen. Even now, his book is a record of an amazing adventure and reflects on a journey of lasting importance. Who knows? Even hundreds of years later it may still be inspiring the next great explorer.

Discussion

1. How do you think Marco Polo affected the life of Christopher Columbus?

2. Have you ever been to some place new and different? Tell what was new or different about it. Did you like it?

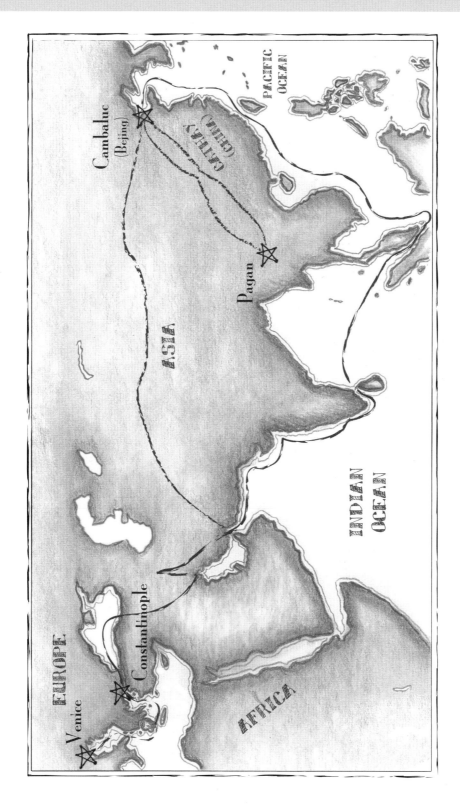

Timeline Review

Put things in perspective. Place Marco Polo's figure on the timeline in the year 1300, which was around the time his book, *The Travels of Marco Polo*, became available. Look at the other events before, during, and after this year.

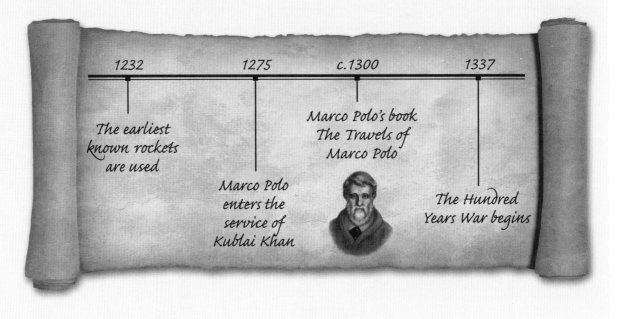

1232 — The earliest known rockets are used

1275 — Marco Polo enters the service of Kublai Khan

c.1300 — Marco Polo's book The Travels of Marco Polo

1337 — The Hundred Years War begins

Activity

1. Either by looking in a reference book, at the library or (with your parents' permission) online, find out what Chinese writing looks like. Try to draw one or two characters from their alphabet. Marco Polo must have seen this language. Do you think it would be difficult to learn? If so, tell why you think it would be difficult.

2. The food cooked and eaten in China is very unique. Look in the cookbook, *Eat Your Way Around the World* and find a recipe from China. Together with your family, make one or more recipes.

   Have you ever eaten in a Chinese restaurant? How is the food different there from what you usually eat?

Wordscramble

Here is a list of scrambled words that relate to the profile you read about Marco Polo. Unscramble the letters and write the words correctly.

1. prxoeler _____
2. onjeyru _____
3. aedvrunte _____
4. hatCya _____
5. balKiu hnaK _____

6. apncait _____
7. obko _____
8. eamspakmr _____
9. maersd _____
10. fawayra _____

Cloze

After reading the passage, try to fill in the blanks with words that make sense about Marco Polo. When you are finished, look at the story to find the words that were used in the passage.

As a matter of fact, Marco's life was filled with _____ new things.

He stayed in _____ for 17 years doing various jobs for Kublai

Khan. Everywhere he went, he _____ the people carefully and

tried to _____ as much as he could about them and their language,

_____, and how they lived and worked. When he left China to

return home, he remembered all the _____, _____, and

_____ he had seen.

True or False

After reading his profile, decide whether you think each of the following statements about Marco Polo and his travels is true or false.

1. _____ Kublai Khan did not like the Polo brothers very much.

2. _____ Marco Polo began his journeys when he was an old man.

3. _____ Marco told his stories to a man he met in prison.

4. _____ The cities of Cathay had many modern features.

5. _____ Marco stayed in Cathay for 17 years.

Marco Polo Word Search

```
X M Y S Y V F A R A W A Y M S W B J J
M T K I E F S A P O B K B A B Q Q C V
K J O U R N E Y T O P M P P S B I U G
L S R M B P R N R O B M H M X D V O Q
S K U B L A I K H A N I A A F D E P C
Z D Q K T G C O C V X M P K O G U Q D
Z N P H I Z K K A X C A W E U Y W C O
Y G D V I A M E T J F R K R C E Y A C
E O D R E A M S H E M C R S H C B P Q
D U K G Z L J B A O Q O X I N S X T J
H P S H Y B U I Y G H P V M N K V A X
M B E V N O B E X P L O R E R X W I Q
K X D H A O R X M I X L W Y U U R N U
F H Z H F K C M J Q D O Q T G D T T W
K K L S A G R P V Z U L K N O P S E I
```

Word Bank

Captain

Cathay

Kublai Khan

Marco Polo

book

dreams

explorer

faraway

journey

mapmakers

Marco Polo Crossword

Across

2. The name China used to be known by

5. Marco's descriptions of the places he had been helped these people do their job

7. One of these was written about Marco Polo's travels

8. The leader of a ship is called this

9. Another name for a long trip

10. Marco Polo was always meant to be this type of person

Down

1. A word that means very distant

3. The leader of China when the Polo brothers went there

4. Another word for imaginings or hopes

6. Marco's life was filled with this

Johannes Gutenberg

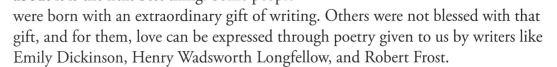

Have you ever read a great book? The kind that you couldn't put down until it was finished? Throughout history, books have entertained, encouraged, and inspired their readers to accomplish the impossible. When people read stories about George Washington, they're encouraged to be brave in the face of great difficulty, and to fight for what is right. Michelangelo painted a ceiling so beautifully that everyone who sees it is completely awed. Artists throughout the world have been inspired by this seemingly unattainable feat, and for those of us who can't travel to Italy to see the Sistine Chapel for ourselves, reading about it is the next best thing. Some people were born with an extraordinary gift of writing. Others were not blessed with that gift, and for them, love can be expressed through poetry given to us by writers like Emily Dickinson, Henry Wadsworth Longfellow, and Robert Frost.

But until a man named Johannes Gutenberg invented a machine called the printing press, stories and poems like these were not widely known. Until the printing press, all of the books were written by hand. Since writing a book by hand took so much time, books were rare and precious things. Only very wealthy people had enough money to buy them. But when the printing press started producing books by the dozens, they became much more affordable – and suddenly ordinary people could learn about extraordinary things.

Through years of experimentation, failure, and discovery, Gutenberg made the first usable printing press in the 14th century. He was not the first man to come up with the idea, but he was the first to work hard enough and long enough to make it happen. The invention seems simple to us today, but it would be very complicated to someone who had nothing to compare his ideas to. The press consisted of a mold in which letters were made from metal. Those letters were arranged in a frame, and then an oil-based ink was smoothed over them. Then paper was pressed on top.

These days books are taken for granted. We have access to knowledge about pretty much anything in the palms of our hands. All a person has to do is find a public library. The next time you read a great book, or walk into a library, just remember it wasn't always so easy.

Discussion

1. How do you think your life would be different if books were still made by hand?

2. If you could only have one book, which one would it be? Why?

Timeline Review

Put things in perspective. Place Johannes Gutenberg's figure on the timeline in the year 1440, which was when he invented the first usable printing press. Look at the other events before, during, and after this year.

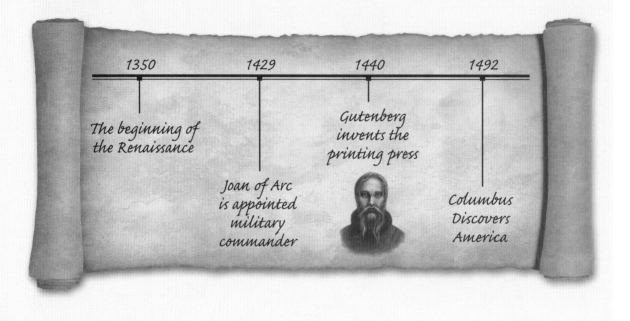

Activity

Using printing stamps and ink that can be obtained at a craft store, make a card or a design for a friend or family member.

Wordscramble

Here is a list of scrambled words that relate to the profile you read about Johannes Gutenberg. Unscramble the letters and write the words correctly.

1. okosb _____
2. eanridg _____
3. eotpry _____
4. gtpnirin sresp _____
5. ivtenoinn _____

6. rteelts _____
7. aaferlfodb _____
8. ppare _____
9. wkeogendl _____
10. biarylr _____

Sequencing

After reading the profile, put Johannes Gutenberg's steps for printing in order. Use the numbers 1–4.

A. _____ Oil based ink was smoothed over the letters.

B. _____ Metal letters were made in a mold.

C. _____ Paper was pressed over the letters.

D. _____ The letters were arranged in a frame.

Cloze

After reading the profile, try to fill in the blanks with words that make sense about Johannes Gutenberg. When you are finished, look at the story to find the words that were used in the passage.

But until a man named Johannes Gutenberg invented a _____ called the printing press, _____ and _____ like these were not widely known. Until the printing press, all of the books were written by _____. Since writing a book by hand took so much time, books were rare and precious things. Only very _____ people had enough _____ to buy them. But when the printing press started producing books by the dozens, they became much more affordable – and suddenly _____ people could learn about extraordinary things.

Johannes Gutenberg Word Search

```
S  E  I  A  F  F  O  R  D  A  B  L  E  B  X  G  K  P  D
N  F  N  A  L  C  V  B  N  P  P  F  T  O  M  P  G  O  K
G  N  V  X  I  I  E  D  X  R  B  K  V  O  B  H  U  E  N
U  Q  E  A  B  E  G  I  C  I  X  Z  P  K  D  J  S  T  O
V  K  N  A  R  I  A  R  K  N  J  U  W  S  D  S  P  R  W
R  E  T  H  A  M  T  E  C  T  U  W  G  T  F  Q  X  Y  L
T  M  I  K  R  B  V  A  W  I  W  C  L  V  R  X  J  F  E
K  V  O  D  Y  X  W  D  X  N  X  W  T  D  B  M  I  K  D
D  Y  N  U  T  A  K  I  W  G  T  U  D  A  Z  R  P  N  G
M  R  O  N  T  A  G  N  N  P  J  P  B  J  N  E  A  V  E
Y  Z  J  G  R  R  N  G  N  R  N  Q  J  P  Z  R  P  X  U
G  M  P  S  J  D  M  L  B  E  S  P  C  S  A  G  E  F  N
S  J  F  Y  P  E  W  S  S  I  A  G  N  P  I  R  G  H
J  L  E  T  T  E  R  S  X  S  G  D  R  D  Q  G  B  A  W
K  X  N  L  T  G  Q  S  X  P  L  I  I  C  J  Z  O  U  S
```

Word Bank

affordable

books

invention

knowledge

letters

library

paper

poetry

printingpress

reading

Johannes Gutenberg Crossword

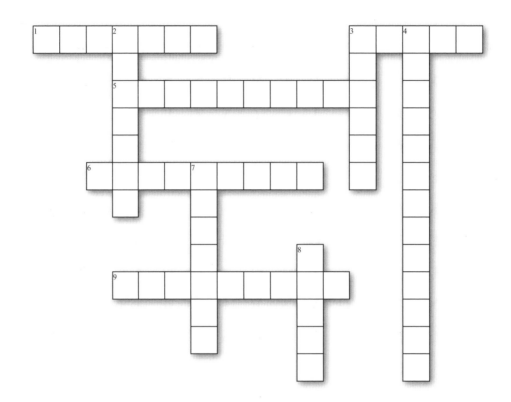

Across

1. A place where books are kept

3. Books are printed on this

5. What something is called when people who are not wealthy are able to buy it

6. One of the most important things a person can get from reading books

9. What something is called when someone figures out a way to make it for the first time

Down

2. This is the next best thing to going, doing, and seeing things for ourselves

3. Some people express love through this type of writing

4. Johannes Gutenberg's invention

7. The things that make up words

8. Gutenberg's printing press made these available to everyone

Leonardo da Vinci

Leonardo da Vinci was a rare man with a very rare gift. Was he an inventor, an artist, or a scientist? He was so special that a new description was coined just for him. If you ever hear the phrase "Renaissance Man" you might also hear the name Leonardo da Vinci. A Renaissance Man is a person who excels in many different areas of the arts and sciences, and da Vinci was exactly that. He was an expert in anatomy, science, math, art, architecture, music, writing, and inventing. Leonardo da Vinci loved to use his mind to ponder, observe, and invent. He explored life through thinking, and enjoyed finding ways to prove or discredit common truths of his time.

Part of his creativity was the ability to see what others might miss. When Leonardo was 51 years old, he began painting a portrait which took four years to complete. But the long hours were worth it in the end because that painting, the *Mona Lisa*, is considered by some to be the most famous painting in the world. One of the reasons it is so popular, besides Leonardo's special talent, is the emotion he captured in this painting. Instead of the blank, elegant look that was common during those days, the lady in this painting is wearing a mysterious expression on her face. It seems as though she might be thinking about a secret. After finally finishing this wonderful painting, Leonardo could never part with it.

Unfortunately, Leonardo started many projects that he never finished. His genius was almost a problem, because he would often get distracted by a new idea before he could finish the project he was working on. This fact has led some people to believe that he refused to give up the *Mona Lisa* simply because he had not yet finished it. But others believe that he grew to love it during the four years he spent creating it. We will never really know why he kept the *Mona Lisa*, but we do know that it stayed with him during his many adventures and travels.

Da Vinci spent the last three years of his life in France, and during that time he finally sold the *Mona Lisa* to his friend, the king. After Leonardo's death in 1519 he was laid to rest in the St. Hubert Chapel in France. *Mona Lisa* was placed in the Louvre museum in Paris, where she will most likely remain forever. She sits behind a layer of bulletproof glass, on display for all to see and admire.

Many have said that da Vinci was ahead of his time. He was fascinated with flight and made drawings of several flying machines, including a helicopter and a hang glider. Among many other things, he thought of a way to use solar energy to heat water, and designed a very primitive submarine. Most of his ideas were never built, but it's interesting to think about what he might have invented with the knowledge and technology we have today. What could one of the greatest minds in history have done in the world as we now know it?

Discussion

1. Leonardo da Vinci was an explorer of ideas and a problem solver. Can you think of any ways that he resembles explorers like John Smith?

2. If you have an opportunity to look at a picture of the *Mona Lisa*, describe her expression. What do you imagine she's thinking or feeling?

Timeline Review

Put things in perspective. Place Leonardo da Vinci's figure on the timeline in the year 1503, which was when he began painting the *Mona Lisa*. Look at the other events before, during, and after this year.

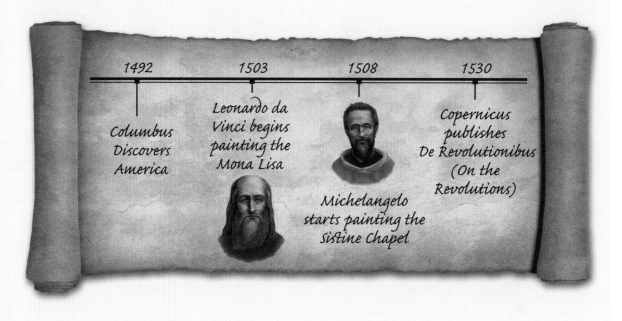

Activity

Have you ever thought about inventing something? An invention can be something that no one has thought of making before, but sometimes it is simply an improvement on something that has already been made. Spend some time thinking about what you would like to invent if you could. Then, make a drawing or build a model that shows what your invention would look like, and what it would do.

Wordscramble

Here is a list of scrambled words that relate to the profile you read about Leonardo da Vinci. Unscramble the letters and write the words correctly.

1. nrtionve _____
2. itsart _____
3. nitcsties _____
4. knightni _____
5. tivyirtaec _____

6. gpinanit _____
7. idaetsdcrt _____
8. oMna sLia _____
9. usmuem _____
10. iardme _____

True or False

After reading his profile, decide whether each of the following statements about Leonardo da Vinci is true or false.

1. _____ Leonardo da Vinci is a good example of a Renaissance Man.

2. _____ None of Leonardo's paintings ever became famous.

3. _____ Sometimes Leonardo would get distracted before he could finish a problem.

4. _____ Leonardo sold the *Mona Lisa* to the King of France.

5. _____ Leonardo was buried in England.

Cloze

After reading the profile, try to fill in the blanks with words that make sense about Leonardo da Vinci. When you are finished, look at the story to find the words that were used in the passage.

Part of his creativity was the _____ to see what others might miss.

When Leonardo was 51 years old, he began painting a _____ which

took four _____ to complete. But the long hours were worth it in the

end because that painting, the *Mona Lisa*, is considered by some to be the most

_____ painting in the world. One of the reasons it is so popular, besides

Leonardo's special talent, is the _____ he captured in this painting.

Instead of the blank, elegant look that was _____ during those days, the

lady in this painting is wearing a mysterious _____ on her face. It seems

like she might be thinking about a special _____. After finally finishing

this wonderful painting, Leonardo could never part with it.

Leonardo da Vinci Word Search

```
C L Z V B W L Z F S C Y F F M F Z R W
A R E H Y R C F O Y H P D Q M H R L V
R G A N A Y R D T G N E D R R Z G B I
T G N Q A A E M U S E U M Z V E Q C N
I J U M Y V A F Q R B T G W S K H B V
S Z Q O U C T J Z N U A N K U W D F E
T Q A N L S I R P T H I N K I N G S N
V Y H A B T V X P A I N T I N G Q Y T
B B J L S M I M N P K K C P W E O B O
P N N I S W T E U O E T M X R I Y J R
U J W S X S Y G U H R R J B R B C T O
L J R A J D D I S T R A C T E D W A I
S K X Q U U X P U H L P L X H E P Z R
K P R M N S H U A S C I E N T I S T O
H W K Q F S U A D M I R E X I U X M O
```

Word Bank

inventor	painting
artist	distracted
scientist	Mona Lisa
thinking	museum
creativity	admire

Leonardo da Vinci Crossword

Across

1. A word for what often happened to Leonardo when he thought of a new idea

8. Leonardo da Vinci's most famous painting

9. What a person is called when he comes up with new ideas for making or doing things

10. The way that Leonardo explored life

Down

2. A person who explores things in nature and science

3. A word that means to appreciate or think highly of

4. A place where people can go to look at famous art or unusual things

5. A type of art that involves using color

6. Leonardo's ability to see what others might miss helped with this

7. A person who skillfully uses his talents; what Leonardo was mainly known as

Michelangelo

Art was a way of thinking for Michelangelo, and he saw life through symbols. He believed that everything had meaning, and that he had a special destiny. From the very beginning Michelangelo had a style all his own -- a unique vision for his artwork.

When Michelangelo was a boy toward the end of the 15th century, he became the student of an artist named Ghirlandaio. Early in his studies, Ghirlandaio realized the gift that Michelangelo had. He also realized that even though young and inexperienced, the child's talent was far greater than his own. Because of this, it might be easy to assume that life for this young genius was full of praise and acclaim, but the world can be a funny place. Michelangelo's teacher had a quick temper, and he felt threatened by his student's great gift. He didn't want to admit that someone so young could have so much more talent. Fortunately for both of them, Michelangelo stayed with Ghirlandaio for less than a year.

After leaving this unhappy situation, he began studies at Bertoldo's academy. There he was first exposed to the art of sculpting, and today Michelangelo is thought of as one of the greatest sculptors of all time. Even though he loved sculpting, every area of art and design greatly interested him, and he excelled at them all. Each of his works, whether in painting, drawing, or sculpture, captured emotion and life, and he used every part of his creations to reveal character.

When Michelangelo was thirty years old, he was commissioned by Pope Julius II to paint the ceiling of a church in Rome called the Sistine Chapel. The church alone is a work of art. It is an ancient building with enough character and beauty to inspire great creativity. Many people who visit the Sistine Chapel and see Michelangelo's masterpiece are awed, and sense immediately that they are standing in the presence of greatness. Clearly, that kind of admiration can only happen when something is so unique and powerful that it will never be duplicated. Michelangelo's vision for the Sistine Chapel was a masterpiece that will be revered forever. His accomplishment is considered the single greatest achievement in art ever completed by one person. He never allowed others to help him with the enormous task because he did not trust anyone else to paint as he wanted. All in all, it took Michelangelo four years of painstaking labor, lying on his back high in the air on a scaffold, to finish painting his masterpiece on the ceiling of the Sistine Chapel. Ironically though, he did not think of himself as a painter, yet his most famous work is a painting.

Architecture, poetry, painting, sculpting, and drawing were all areas in which Michelangelo excelled. History remembers him as a true Renaissance Man, whose masterpieces and legacy have proven to be timeless.

Discussion

1. Michelangelo's creativity showed up in many different forms such as architecture, poetry, painting, sculpting, and drawing. Think of your family members and make a list of 2 or 3 ways that they show creativity differently.

2. Try to find a picture of Michelangelo's painting on the ceiling of the Sistine Chapel. What story do you think the painting tells? What part of the painting do you think is the most important?

ALPS

Arezzo ☆

ITALY

ADRIATIC SEA

☆ Rome

Sistine Chapel

TYRRHENIAN
SEA

MEDITERRANEAN SEA

Timeline Review

Put things in perspective. Place Michelangelo's figure on the timeline in the year 1508, which was when he started painting the Sistine Chapel. Look at the other events before, during and after this year

1503 — Leonardo da Vinci begins painting the Mona Lisa

1508 — Michelangelo starts painting the Sistine Chapel

1530 — Copernicus publishes De Revolutionibus (On the Revolutions)

1547 — Ivan the Terrible is crowned King of Russia

Activity

Tape a piece of plain paper on the bottom of your coffee table. Then lie down under the table and use crayons, colored pencils or watercolor paint to draw and color a picture on the paper.

Wordscramble

Here is a list of scrambled words that relate to the profile you read about Michelangelo. Unscramble the letters and write the words correctly.

1. rta _____

2. slbsyom _____

3. teidysn _____

4. ttnlea _____

5. puteculrs _____

6. pCehal sntSiei _____

7. clffadso _____

8. dgriawn _____

9. naipgitn _____

10. eclgini _____

Cloze

After reading the profile, try to fill in the blanks with words that make sense about Michelangelo. When you are finished, look at the story to find the words that were used in the passage.

After leaving this _____ situation, he began studies at Bertlodo's academy. There he was first exposed to the art of _____, and today Michelangelo is thought of as one of the _____ sculptors of all time. But even though he _____ sculpting, every area of art and _____ greatly interested him, and he excelled at them all. Each of his works, whether a painting, _____, or sculpture, captured emotion and life, and he used every part of his creations to reveal _____.

True or False

After reading his profile, decide whether each of the following statements about Michelangelo is true or false.

1. _____ Michelangelo studied with the artist named Ghirlandaio for many years.

2. _____ Michelangelo was very good at sculpting.

3. _____ Many people helped Michelangelo paint the ceiling in the Sistine Chapel.

4. _____ Michelangelo stood on scaffolding to paint his masterpiece in the Sistine Chapel.

5. _____ Michelangelo excelled in many areas of art.

Michelangelo Word Search

```
O Q B C Z R L S Y M B O L S L V H L M
Y I W P I T O L X D J J Z C M L Z P S
U D R A W I N G M F A M E U F L R K C
F E G R W R X T N B I R R L N X P R A
H S U S I S T I N E C H A P E L R N F
F T Y O U U X W A N W B P T T M I J F
O I N M U T S U P W W Y L U X N M H O
E N O A E V V T A L E N T R K P M M L
M Y A J C A I H I Z H M Y E W N S L D
C E I L I N G P N X V F O D B U M I G
X B K E X L P L T X K B U M C H R Q P
L C G T H E O K I E M Q Q T Z J C K I
H S Y W I Y W U N O C H H B O A R T T
B S P O Y L F S G M Y W E N J Y M O R
N G H T A O W I E B I T I E H U C V A
```

Word Bank

Sistine Chapel

art

ceiling

destiny

drawing

painting

scaffold

sculpture

symbols

talent

Michelangelo Crossword

Across

2. A type of art usually done with a pencil

4. A special gift or ability to do something; something Michelangelo had a great deal of

6. The part of the Sistine Chapel that Michelangelo painted

7. Usually a carving made out of stone

8. A type of art that involves the use of color

9. Things that stand for, or remind people of, other things

Down

1. The church where Michelangelo's most famous painting is located

2. A word that refers to what is "meant to be" for a person

3. An area of study that includes drawing, painting, and sculpture

5. A raised platform that Michelangelo used to paint the Sistine Chapel

William Shakespeare

"Be not afraid of greatness: Some are born great, others achieve greatness, and some have greatness thrust upon 'em."

-Shakespeare

W illiam Shakespeare was one of those people who was born great. His greatness was not taught to him. He didn't have to work at it, he just was.

Shakespeare was born in Stratford, a small town in England. One of eight children, he attended the King Edward Grammar School. After his childhood education, Shakespeare never attended a university or needed any other form of higher education.

Shakespeare wrote thirty-seven plays, one hundred and fifty sonnets (which are a type of poetry,) and a few other types of poems. Shakespeare had a wonderful sense of humor, which often showed up in his writing. He must have enjoyed writing comedies more than anything else, because 17 of his plays are that type. The rest of his plays are histories and tragedies. Among the tragedies is his most famous play, *Romeo and Juliet*. It is a grand story of two young people who find themselves caught in a forbidden love.

For William Shakespeare, writing became art through words like these:

"But soft! What light through yonder window breaks? It is the east, and Juliet is the sun."

-Romeo

"This bud of love, by summer's ripening breath may prove a beauteous flower when next we meet."

-Juliet

It seems strange how the choice and arrangement of words can change a sentence from being average to excellent. Many poems have the same meaning. The writers were trying to convey the same thought and yet, some poems are considered to be magnificent works of art, while others dull, or merely acceptable. The difference is in the way the words are fit together. Shakespeare had a gift for writing. His arrangement of words touched people in a way that others have tried to duplicate for 400 years. Some have come close, but so far no one has been able to reach his level.

People in that day went to the theatre as a way to escape normal life. It was all they had in the form of entertainment. They came to see Shakespeare's plays and forget about their own hardships. Shakespeare understood human emotion and skillfully portrayed life's struggles. If you've ever watched a play by Shakespeare, or read one, you start to realize that you know the characters. Some of them you'll find in yourself, and some you'll find in the people around you. The community loved Shakespeare's work because they could identify with his characters. They came to laugh; they came to cry, and to appreciate a new kind of art.

During his time Shakespeare, was highly thought of and well liked. No one imagined however, that he would someday be considered the greatest English writer of all time. Shakespeare's plays have been imitated time and time again throughout the world. Movies have been made about him, and about most of his plays. He is the most quoted author in the English-speaking world.

If you ever happen to be in Stratford, England be sure to visit the Holy Trinity Church, where Shakespeare was laid to rest in the year 1616. He died on April 23rd, which also happens to be his birthday. Even in his death Shakespeare left us something to remember. Written in his own words, on his tombstone is this:

> *Good friend, for Jesus' sake forebear*
>
> *To dig the dust enclosed here!*
>
> *Blest be the man that spares these stones,*
>
> *And cursed be he that moves my bones.*

Discussion

1. Shakespeare is an example of someone who seems destined, or born with the abilities, to be a great writer. Have you ever known anyone who seemed born with skills that other people had to learn? Can you think of anything that you were born with the ability to do well? Do you think it is just as good to learn to do something well?

2. The language used by Shakespeare was English, though it seems very different from the way we speak today. Reread the following line from *Romeo and Juliet* and tell your teacher what you think it means:
   "But soft! What light through yonder window breaks? It is the east, and Juliet is the sun."

   Do you like the English used by Shakespeare? Why or why not?

Activity

During Shakespeare's time, acting companies were small. Because of this, one actor might have to play several roles. Sometimes boys had to act out the roles of female characters.

Choose a character from a story you know and act the story out from his or her point of view. Then choose another character from the same story and act it out again, from the new character's point of view. You may want to act out a story with a good guy and a bad guy, and play both parts.

Timeline Review

Put things in perspective. Place William Shakespeare's figure on the timeline in the year 1595, which was around the time he wrote *Romeo and Juliet*. Look at the other events before, during, and after this year.

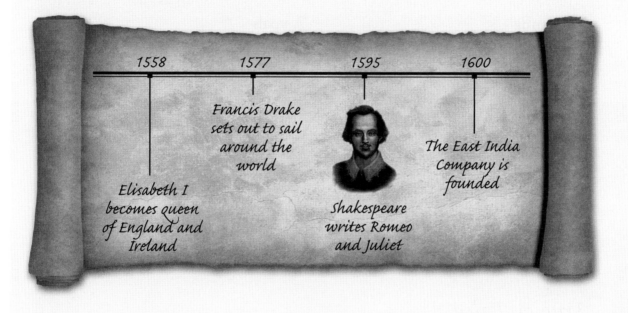

1558   1577   1595   1600

Francis Drake
sets out to sail
around the
world

The East India
Company is
founded

Elisabeth I
becomes queen
of England and
Ireland

Shakespeare
writes Romeo
and Juliet

Wordscramble

Here is a list of scrambled words that relate to the profile you read about William Shakespeare. Unscramble the letters and write the words correctly.

1. rSrfottad _____

2. nldanEg _____

3. moecidse _____

4. trsoihise _____

5. tgiaseerd _____

6. truhoa _____

7. ypals _____

8. seosnnt _____

9. imliWal _____

10. herTaet _____

True or False

After reading William Shakespeare's profile, decide whether the following statements are true or false.

1. _____ Shakespeare learned to write when he was at a university.

2. _____ Shakespeare wrote more tragedies than any other kind of play.

3. _____ A sonnet is a type of poem.

4. _____ Shakespeare's plays were only enjoyed by kings and queens, not regular people.

5. _____ Shakespeare is the most quoted author in the English-speaking world.

Cloze

After reading the profile, try to fill in the blanks with words that make sense about William Shakespeare. When you are finished, look at the story to find the words that were used in the passage.

Shakespeare wrote thirty-seven plays, one hundred and fifty sonnets (which are a type of poetry,) and a few other types of _____. Shakespeare had a wonderful sense of _____, which often showed up in his writing. He must have enjoyed writing _____ more than anything else, because 17 of his plays are that type. The rest of his plays are _____ and _____. Among the tragedies is his most famous play, *Romeo and Juliet*. It is a grand story of two young people who find themselves caught in a forbidden love.

William Shakespeare Word Search

```
M E Q N O D O B T X J H L C S Z U Y U
E B W H I P W O W C E V L Q Z Z U W G
N C K M S T I F R L X O E J A L V O D
G O L J T H L A U T H O R T A W C K M
L J M D R H L G P L A Y S R R L F I G
A H V O A I I W G C U L V A R P P O Y
N L N H T S A D A O K F K G M R J K H
D S R U F T M X B M W S Z E E T P N A
G I E A O O D Q F E V O Q D Z H L G T
S Y P S R R Y B K D I N B I T E M J D
G H S V D I U S O I A N B E Y A R N M
E Z C J V E Y X R E K E M S L T V W Z
J Z Z O O S I A S S F T W S N R N L A
D O M P Z Q T M K L Y S T M M E Y P S
M D E T K M K Q V K H B Y Y C I H Z E
```

Word Bank

Stratford	author
England	plays
comedies	sonnets
histories	William
tragedies	theatre

William Shakespeare Crossword

Across

2. A person who writes something
5. A type of play that tells about things that happened in the past
6. A type of writing that is meant to be acted out
8. The country where Shakespeare lived
9. The type of play that must have been Shakespeare's favorite

Down

1. The town where Shakespeare was born
3. Romeo and Juliet is this type of play
4. Shakespeare's first name
7. A place where plays are acted out
10. Shakespeare wrote 150 of these

John Smith

Fmm the very beginning, John Smith wanted adventure. He grew up daydreaming of far off places and dangerous journeys. He wanted to see as much of the world as possible. Wherever his life took him, instead of following a leader, he became the leader.

When John was 16, he left his home in London to become a soldier. Everywhere Smith went, he stirred confidence in his abilities and promotion seemed to follow. Altogether, he spent six years of his life as a soldier. When his days in the armed forces were over, Smith traveled all through Europe and Northern Africa. A part of the young hero's dream came true during that time, because he got to see a small piece of the world. After his travels, he went back home to England.

John Smith's most challenging adventure came next. He was 27 years old when he sailed to Jamestown, Virginia, and helped establish the first English colony in the New World. People sailed to the New World for many reasons. Some of the colonists believed that they would find gold in Jamestown, but money held little value in John Smith's eyes. He understood the difficulties of building a new colony in a foreign land. Most of the settlers with whom he traveled did not.

Unlike Captain Smith, nearly half of the people who came to the New World were of England's upper class. They did not think they needed to work for their food, or help build the city. They simply expected the work to be done for them. It would soon become apparent to them that this was not the case. At one point while Smith was leader of the colony, he made a declaration that "those who do not work, do not eat." Smith valued hard work, and knew that it would make the difference between life and death for these people. This was an unpopular stand, but rarely did he think of himself during his days in Jamestown.

In England, only those who were born of noble blood were given roles of leadership, but in the New World that changed. Smith was not born of noble blood, but in Jamestown nobility of heart made a new type of leader. Although he led Jamestown for only one year, during that time he probably saved the colonists from starvation by strictly rationing the few supplies they had. He insisted that every person do his or her part, and he required the people to grow whatever they could. Changes like this brought order to the colony, and helped it survive a very difficult time.

John Smith's natural leadership skills were also noticed by those who were not from the colony. During Smith's time in Virginia, Chief Powhatan of the nearby Powhatan Indians would never wage a full war against the English. The Indian chief respected John Smith for his courage and his confidence. Unfortunately, after only a year of leading the colony John was badly burned by a sack of gunpowder. It was attached to his waist when it exploded. His injuries needed better treatment than Jamestown could offer, so in 1609 Smith left the colony where he had worked so hard. He sailed back to England, and never returned to Jamestown.

Not surprisingly, after Smith left the colony suffered greatly. The next few months were known to them as "the starving time." When Chief Powhatan found out that Smith had left Jamestown, he no longer had a reason to be merciful to the struggling colonists. It took many years before the Virginia colony returned to strength and success.

John Smith spent the majority of his remaining days in England. Some of the history that he wrote during that time had not been recorded by anyone else. He also made very valuable maps of Virginia and the New England area that stayed in use for many years. John Smith died at the age of 51. Why did he never return to Jamestown? Were the memories too bitter? We can only speculate, but a statue now stands in Jamestown, Virginia, built for a dignified and confident man. His chin is slightly lifted, and he's facing the ocean from where he came. This statue represents one of America's first heroes, John Smith.

Discussion

1. Why do you think John Smith was an unpopular leader?

2. Why do you think John Smith never returned to Jamestown?

Timeline Review

Put things in perspective. Place John Smith's figure on the timeline in the year 1606, which was when he sailed to Jamestown. Look at the other events before, during, and after this year.

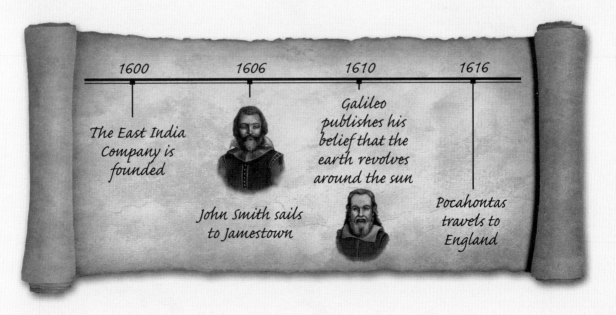

1600 — The East India Company is founded

1606 — John Smith sails to Jamestown

1610 — Galileo publishes his belief that the earth revolves around the sun

1616 — Pocahontas travels to England

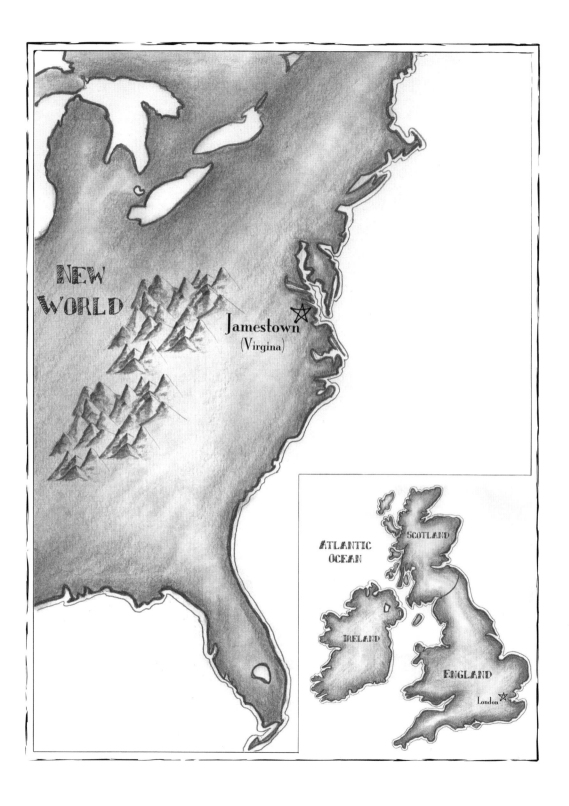

Activity

Try planting and growing a vegetable of your choice with your parent's help. If it is too chilly outdoors, put your plant in a container inside the house. Be sure to put it in a place where there is plenty of sunlight. Don't worry if you have never tried gardening before – many of the Jamestown colonists had never worked with plants and soil before they came to the New World.

Cloze

After reading the profile, try to fill in the blanks with words that make sense about John Smith. When you are finished, look at the story to find the words that were used in the passage.

This man's natural _____ skills were also noticed by those who were not from the colony. During Smith's time in Virginia, _____ _____ of the nearby Powhatan Indians would never wage a full war against the English. The Indian chief _____ John Smith for his courage and his confidence. Unfortunately, after only a year of leading the colony John was badly _____ by a sack of gunpowder. It was attached to his waist when it exploded. His injuries needed better _____ than Jamestown could offer, so in 1609 Smith left the colony where he had worked so hard. He sailed back to _____ , and never returned to _____ .

Wordscramble

Here is a list of scrambled words that relate to the profile you read about John Smith. Unscramble the letters and write the words correctly.

1. eruojyns _____
2. roelisd _____
3. oher _____
4. nwsJmoaet _____
5. loycno _____

6. uuprpnloa _____
7. delear _____
8. oylbinti _____
9. ivvsreu _____
10. igirVnia _____

Sequencing

Put the following events in John Smith's life in the proper order. Use the numbers 1–5.

A. _____ John sailed to Virginia when he was 27.

B. _____ He helped establish the first English colony in the New World.

C. _____ When he was a teenager, John Smith left his home in London to become a soldier.

D. _____ He spent some time traveling through Europe and Northern Africa.

E. _____ John became a leader in Jamestown.

John Smith Word Search

```
E N N U N P O P U L A R J D A T G H P
C H J W O R B J Q S D V S D G B B O T
I L A P B K J O M P H Q Q T S J C V L
R W M J I Y H U M S O R C T U I H T X
A X E U L R I R J B C H S R N N K Z
L Z S X I R D N E Q N E N T V Q Y M I
X I T Y T T D E C E I R N V I O H S O
O P O L Y C O Y R H I O K I V F X C I
Z V W P G M S S O L D I E R E I C G G
J Z N J C O L O N Y S B F G I M Q L A
I W Q Y W B A M V Y W T P I W I Z Y O
P I P O I R G H V H O D V N P S Q I P
L E A D E R R T D P A P W I Z Y G Q P
C C E V B M Y F X W S N G A F Y Q T X
F Q A X C Y M G Y G B N R V L R V L K
```

Word Bank

Jamestown	leader
Virginia	nobility
colony	soldier
hero	survive
journeys	unpopular

John Smith Crossword

Across

2. A person who is brave or courageous
3. The state where Jamestown is located
6. A word used when something is not well liked
9. This was the first English colony in the New World
10. A settlement in a new country

Down

1. Someone who is in the army
4. John Smith helped Jamestown do this during a very difficult time
5. A word that means long trips
7. Someone who is in charge
8. A word that describes John Smith's excellent character and values

Galileo

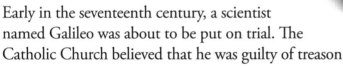

People throughout history who made a difference, the ones we read about today, were the kind of people who stood up for what they believed in. They didn't follow the crowd or live quiet, normal lives. They were brave and courageous men and women. From time to time many of them probably wished they were more like everyone else, because it would have made life much easier. But it is because of these people and their sacrifices that our world has grown so in knowledge and understanding.

Early in the seventeenth century, a scientist named Galileo was about to be put on trial. The Catholic Church believed that he was guilty of treason because he claimed that the earth was not the center of the universe, as everyone at that time thought. Instead, he said that the earth revolved around the sun. This was not a new idea, and others who had suggested it in the past had suffered greatly. Galileo knew this, and so he had a difficult choice to make. He could go home and give up the argument, or he could stay in Rome and fight for what he believed to be true. Galileo decided to stay.

Because of his courage, the door was opened for questions and new thoughts. Before Galileo came along, most people simply believed what they had been told. They assumed that whatever the great philosopher, Aristotle, had written was the truth. Galileo, on the other hand, questioned everything until he could make an educated decision for himself. Sometimes he would agree with an existing idea, and other times he would create a whole new theory.

When Galileo was about 46, he began using a small telescope that could make objects seem thirty times closer. With this telescope he studied the heavens, and was the first person to see that the moon is not smooth like everyone thought. It is covered with huge craters. He then discovered that Venus' appearance changes just like the moon's. This led to further observations which proved that Venus revolves around the sun. He had finally proven his theory that the sun, not the earth, is the center of our solar system! But Galileo gave credit where it was due when he said, "I give thanks to God, who has made me the first to look upon these marvelous things."

Sir Isaac Newton, who many consider the most influential scientist of all time, was born on the day that Galileo died. Newton left us with this very famous quote: "If I have been able to see further, it is only because I stood on the shoulders of giants." He was referring to scientists like Galileo, who questioned common beliefs and suggested new ideas. Through his studies, Isaac Newton proved that Galileo was far ahead of his time. He contributed much to the world during his time, but more importantly Galileo completely changed the study of science.

Discussion

1. What do you think Sir Isaac Newton meant when he said, "If I have been able to see further, it is only because I stood on the shoulders of giants."

2. Have you ever had to stand up for something you believe in? What happened?

Timeline Review

Put things in perspective. Place Galileo's figure on the timeline in the year 1610, which was when he published his belief that the earth revolves around the sun. Look at the other events before, during, and after this year.

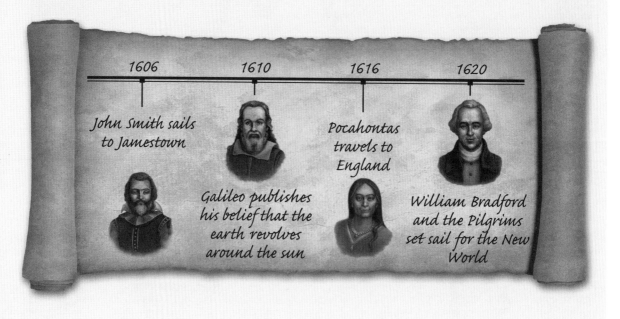

| 1606 | 1610 | 1616 | 1620 |

John Smith sails to Jamestown

Galileo publishes his belief that the earth revolves around the sun

Pocahontas travels to England

William Bradford and the Pilgrims set sail for the New World

Activity

Galileo's telescope made objects seem 30 times closer than they were. Use a telescope or binoculars to look at several objects. Draw a picture of how the objects look using just your eyes, and then draw what you see when you look through the telescope or binoculars. What did you notice with the telescope or binoculars that you did not see using just your eyes?

Wordscramble

Here is a list of scrambled words that relate to the profile you read about Galileo. Unscramble the letters and write the words correctly.

1. ecsistint _____

2. lirat _____

3. reotnas _____

4. rvuisnee _____

5. Alirettso _____

6. ecopleset _____

7. rsrctae _____

8. rnatbissoveo _____

9. nteNow _____

10. fseeilb _____

True or False

After reading the profile about Galileo, tell whether you think the following statements are true or false.

1. _____ Galileo believed the Earth is the center of the universe.

2. _____ Newton gave credit to the scientists who came before him.

3. _____ Galileo appears to have believed in God.

4. _____ Galileo had little effect on the study of science.

5. _____ Galileo saw that Venus revolves around the sun.

Cloze

After reading the profile, try to fill in the blanks with words that make sense about Galileo. When you are finished, look at the story to find the words that were used in the passage.

When Galileo was about 46, he began using a small _____ that could make objects seem thirty times closer. With this telescope he studied the _____, and was the first person to see that the moon is not _____ like everyone thought. It is covered with huge craters. He then discovered that Venus' _____ changes just like the moon's. This led to further observations which proved that Venus _____ around the sun. He had finally proven his _____ that the sun, not the earth, is the _____ of our solar system! But Galileo gave credit where it was due when he said, "I give _____ to God, who has made me the first to look upon these marvelous things."

Galileo Word Search

```
K Q O B P Y M K A Q T D T S N O W C O
P I B W F T C P V N S O Y C J B R D E
A A N Q J K F E E D S L C I D S H T I
E Z J B D N A U J L H A Z E J E S E Q
U J Y B I T S Q F C U F N B R K L D
Q N F P X R E Y R Z X U I T W V L E J
N S N A R I S T O T L E R I Q A C S G
D I E O V A F B E L I E F S N T O C V
B Y W V M L T G K B M G W T L I E O R
D R T I A D A B B C A U N J P O X P W
L T O U I U N I V E R S E V O N G E E
M S N O S U M Z I C R A T E R S F Z J
T R E A S O N F J F I Q V R W Z E E Y
H I D S B W C T G R T E O S N P L U Z
C Q Z Y D L L Z C F D I Q Y M S W B F
```

Word Bank

scientist
trial
treason
universe
Aristotle

telescope
craters
observations
Newton
beliefs

Galileo Crossword

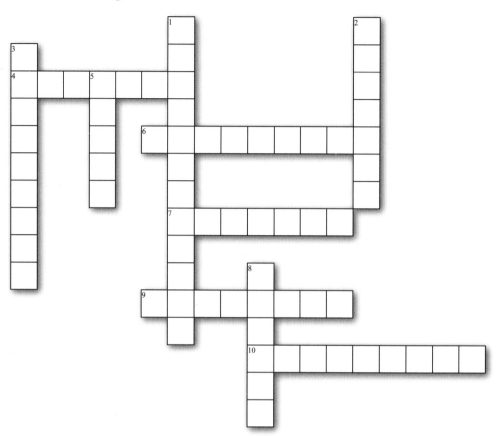

Across

4. Things that Galileo observed on the moon's surface

6. The name of a great philosopher

7. Another word for disloyalty, and the crime that Galileo was accused of

9. All the matter in space, including the Earth

10. The tool that allowed Galileo to explore the heavens

Down

1. What it was called in the Profile when Galileo looked carefully at Venus through his telescope

2. The common things that Galileo questioned when he suggested new ideas

3. A person who explores things in nature and science

5. The name of what happens when someone is charged with a crime and taken to court

8. The man who is considered the most influential scientist of all time

Pocahontas

There once was a Powhatan girl born in the area we now call Virginia. Her father was the chief, and although he had many daughters, she was his favorite. Pochahontas, which means mischievous, was her public name. But her family called her Matoaka, which means playful or frolicsome.

When Pocahontas was about 11 years old, some Englishmen arrived nearby and began building the colony called Jamestown. This colony was not welcomed by the Indians, especially Pocahontas' father. Even so, these new arrivals would someday change the course of her life. She was drawn to the English colony, and throughout most of her life was connected to it in one way or another. Even her father's disapproval could not stop Pocahontas from helping the English through many great difficulties.

The first time Pocahontas met John Smith, he was her father's prisoner. Interestingly, he had been captured while on an expedition to find and meet the great Powhatan chief. After being moved from village to village, never knowing his fate, Smith was finally brought to a meeting in Powhatan's house. Pocahontas watched as the Indians decided what to do with him. After a long time, Powhatan ordered Smith's execution. The Indians placed his head on a large stone, but just as they were about to kill him, Pocahontas laid her head over his, saving him from a terrible fate!

Pocahontas often came to visit John Smith and the rest of the English colony. Many times she brought them food. Captain Smith later said that Pocahontas helped keep the colony alive. While he was governor, Captain Smith received a strange order from King James in England. The English king wanted Smith to offer Powhatan a crown in exchange for his loyalty. In order to become a king, the great chief Powhatan would have to bow down and commit himself to England and the English king. As Captain Smith suspected, even though the chief accepted the crown he was very upset at the thought of bowing to England. Soon after, Powhatan declared that his people would no longer trade with the English, and he forbid Pocahontas to visit the colony.

Captain Smith knew that without trade with the Indians, his people would starve. So when Chief Powhatan acted like he wanted to be friends again, the captain was more than willing. Unfortunately, what looked like an offer of friendship turned out to be an ambush, with Smith and his men surrounded by Indians! However, when the captain fired his gun, the Indians scattered. By that time the tide had gone out, and they were unable to set sail. So Smith and his men decided to rest for the night. Later, Pocahontas appeared with a warning that her father had not given up his plans to kill them, and she told them to leave immediately. At great risk to herself, Pocahontas saved John Smith's life once again! When she snuck away that night, little did she know that they would not see each other again for eight years.

After the men returned to Jamestown, Smith had an accident and was badly burned. As a result, he had to sail back to England to recover. He did not say goodbye to Pocahontas, but she heard that he was no longer among the colonists. The Indians didn't know what to believe. Some said he had gone home, others claimed he was dead. The only thing Pocahontas knew for sure was that she would never set foot in Jamestown again.

Pocahontas now lived with a nearby tribe in the Patawamake village. The new Captain of Jamestown decided to visit the village where he used Pocahontas' kindness against her. She had missed the English and eagerly accepted his invitation to tour their ship. However once on board, even though Captain Argall and his crew treated her like royalty, she was not allowed to leave. Pocahontas never dreamed she would become a prisoner of the English!

When they arrived back in Jamestown, a ransom note was sent to Powhatan. Captain Argall wanted to trade Pocahontas for some English people who had been captured, along with corn, swords, and guns that the Indians had taken. Most importantly, the colonists wanted the war to end. The Chief, however, did not cooperate with Argall's conditions. He released seven of the eight prisoners, and sent only a small amount of corn back. The English were not satisfied, and Pocahontas remained a prisoner.

Weeks, and then months, went by with no response from Powhatan. After awhile, she was sent to live with Reverend Alexander Whitaker on his large farm. While there, Pocahontas began dressing in English blouses and skirts, and was taught about the Christian faith. John Rolfe, who was her teacher, spoke of her great desire to learn about God.

Rolfe's wife and infant daughter had died shortly after coming to Jamestown, and Pocahontas' playful, peaceful spirit helped him through his tragic circumstances. As he taught Pocahontas about the Bible, John Rolfe fell in love with the Indian princess. Rolfe, who was a handsome young man, asked Pocahontas to be his wife and she agreed. At last, because of their marriage, the war between the English and the Powhatan Indians finally ended. It was indeed Pocahontas who brought peace to Jamestown.

In 1615, Pocahontas gave birth to a son named Thomas. Later, when the family visited England, she was viewed as a beautiful and poised woman. The English did not expect such manners from a so-called savage. When John Smith heard of Pocahontas' presence in England, he wrote Queen Anne a letter stating that the Indian princess had come to the aid of Jamestown many times. The Queen was very impressed, and invited her to the palace. No doubt Pocahontas' visit with the Queen was a high point of her time in England.

After several weeks in London, Pocahontas became ill. As a result, the Rolfes moved to a nearby town called Brentford, where she was much happier. There were many more trees and cleaner air, which probably reminded her of home. Meanwhile, John Smith heard that Pocahontas was ill, and decided to visit her. She believed that he had died, so you can imagine how surprised she was to see him! The two old friends talked for some time, and Pocahontas referred to Smith as her "father." They never saw each other again after that day, but when she died Captain Smith grieved for her and declared that he had thought of Pocahontas as his own daughter.

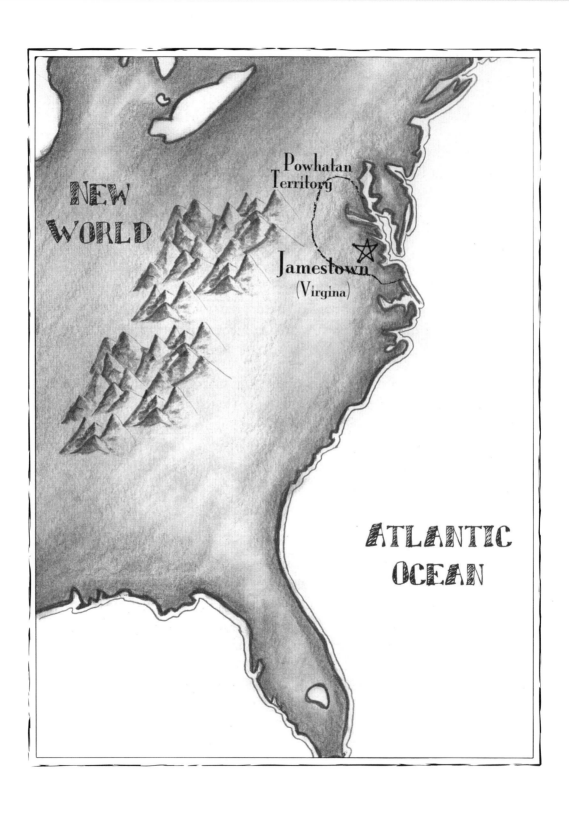

Discussion

1. Why do you think the Powhatan Indians were so hostile toward the English?

2. Pocahontas stood up for what she thought was right no matter what the consequences were. What do you think you would have done if you were in her place?

Timeline Review

Put things in perspective. Place Pocahontas' figure on the timeline in the year 1616, which was when she traveled to England. Look at the other events before, during, and after this year.

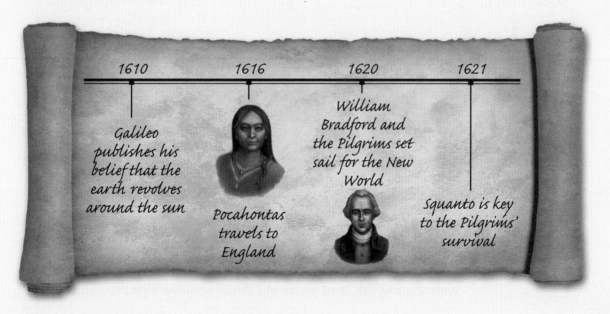

1610	1616	1620	1621

Galileo publishes his belief that the earth revolves around the sun

Pocahontas travels to England

William Bradford and the Pilgrims set sail for the New World

Squanto is key to the Pilgrims' survival

Activity

1. List some of the ways that Pocahontas helped the English settlers.

2. Research the type of housing used by the Powhatan Indians.

Cloze

After reading the profile, try to fill in the blanks with words that make sense about Pocahontas. When you are finished, look at the story to find the words that were used in the passage.

Pocahontas often came to _____ John Smith and the rest of the English colony. Many times she brought them _____. Captain Smith later said that Pocahontas helped keep the colony alive. While he was _____, Captain Smith received a _____ order from King James in England. The English king wanted Smith to offer Powhatan a _____ in exchange for his loyalty. In order to become a king, the great chief Powhatan would have to _____ and commit himself to England and the English king. As Captain Smith suspected, even though the chief accepted the crown he was very _____ at the thought of bowing to England. Soon after, Powhatan declared that his people would no longer _____ with the English, and he forbid Pocahontas to visit the colony.

Wordscramble

Here is a list of scrambled words that relate to the profile you read about Pocahontas. Unscramble the letters and write the words correctly.

1. tahawoPn _____
2. uyflalp _____
3. ncooyl _____
4. heignlp _____
5. suhmba _____

6. rwgnani _____
7. srneipor _____
8. asmrno _____
9. oJnh lfReo _____
10. srienpcs _____

Sequencing

Put the following events from Pocahontas' life in their correct order. Use the numbers 1–5.

A. _____ Powhatan ordered John Smith's execution.

B. _____ John Smith was captured while on an expedition to meet the great chief.

C. _____ Pocahontas laid her head on top of John Smith's, and saved his life.

D. _____ While he was a prisoner, John Smith was moved from village to village.

E. _____ Pocahontas watched as the Indians decided what to do with John Smith.

Pocahontas Word Search

```
S  P  G  O  M  P  A  W  Y  H  H  E  L  P  I  N  G  A  Q
Z  L  Z  M  K  Q  M  Y  P  A  H  A  Q  J  T  Z  K  I  I
J  A  I  W  S  I  B  L  P  D  T  R  R  M  M  A  B  K  X
O  Y  D  B  C  J  U  F  W  E  H  W  F  O  O  D  Z  E  E
H  F  H  D  A  A  S  P  R  I  N  C  E  S  S  C  G  E  V
N  U  D  P  L  E  H  E  E  P  I  A  Z  Q  P  T  W  S  C
R  L  G  P  U  R  C  R  P  P  O  W  H  A  T  A  N  R  O
O  M  D  I  W  K  E  A  H  U  G  W  O  G  Z  F  T  P  L
L  S  D  V  C  P  F  N  O  D  P  R  I  S  O  N  E  R  O
F  V  I  P  A  Q  Q  S  B  D  F  I  R  R  Y  Y  E  C  N
E  W  I  D  C  Z  N  O  L  X  X  P  W  H  Q  U  B  E  Y
B  Y  V  J  S  P  O  M  J  P  W  A  R  N  I  N  G  T  F
T  V  P  M  F  T  R  Z  F  K  B  R  R  H  C  B  X  P  J
V  H  R  O  F  V  C  T  Y  P  K  J  W  Y  P  U  V  T  Q
Z  D  S  R  V  K  W  Q  F  X  H  X  I  Z  M  K  S  D  G
```

Word Bank

Powhatan

playful

colony

helping

ambush

warning

prisoner

ransom

John Rolfe

Princess

Pocahontas Crossword

Across

1. Name of the tribe that Pocahontas came from

4. The name her family called her meant this

7. The type of note that Captain Argall sent to Pocahontas' father

9. The man who taught Pocahontas about God

Down

2. Her father's disapproval did not stop Pocahontas from doing this for the English

3. This is what Pocahontas gave Smith and his men that saved them from her father

4. The daughter of a chief or a king

5. What Pocahontas became on Captain Argall's ship

6. Another word for a trap or surprise attack

8. A settlement in a new country

William Bradford

Meeting in secret, hiding strong beliefs – this could not go on any longer! William Bradford stepped onto a small ship called the *Mayflower* in the year 1620. As he took his first steps inside the ship his thoughts drifted to the future. "What might this New World be like?" he wondered. Would it be everything they hoped? Would they find the peace and refuge they were looking for? As he looked around the small room inside the ship, he lifted his eyes toward the sky and asked God to bless their journey.

William Bradford was among the 102 Pilgrims who sailed from England to the New World on the *Mayflower*. They left their homes and all the things that were familiar to them. Some people even had to leave behind family members who would come to the new land at a later time. Even this parting with loved ones could not turn them away from their purpose. The Pilgrims left England to start a new colony where they could worship God as they desired. Their religious views did not line up with the Church of England's religious views, but their faith was so great that obstacles seemed like nothing. They were known as the Separatists, because they wanted to be separate from the Church of England. King James I kept England under strict rule; differences were not welcome. Therefore the Separatists were mistreated and even attacked at times.

William Bradford wrote this in his journal about leaving England in search of the new world:

"All great and honorable actions are accompanied with great difficulties, and must be both enterprised and overcome with answerable courages. It was granted ye dangers were great, but not desperate; the difficulties were many, but not invincible."

These were not the kind of people to give up easily, but Bradford stood out even among such strong believers. He was known for his bravery, wisdom, and his ability to see past hardships to the rewards ahead. The noble William Bradford was a leader with a strong voice for the 'saints,' as they called themselves. As a matter of fact, he played an important part in every major decision they made.

The saints traveled through the stormy waters of the Atlantic for 66 days. They were all crowded in that small ship, and soon after their departure nearly everyone became horribly seasick. It is hard to imagine their misery. They missed home, they felt sick, and they were crammed into one small room.

They finally reached the shores of America after a long and dangerous journey. William Bradford, among other determined believers, created the Mayflower Compact. Each of the 41 men who signed this document agreed to the laws it established, and thereby created a foundation for the future of the Plymouth government.

The Pilgrims arrived in this new land in December,1620, only to be welcomed by the bitter cold of a New England winter. What did this mean for the brave saints? Nearly all became ill, including Bradford. Within a few months of their arrival half of their company died, and among the dead was their first elected governor, John Carver. Stepping up again to answer the call of duty, Bradford was elected governor in his place. In a fitting tribute to his leadership and service, not one Pilgrim disagreed with his election.

From the faith of this small but determined group of believers came the beginnings of our mighty nation. William Bradford stood as their friend and leader until his death 37 years later.

Discussion

1. If they had known what was to come, do you think the Pilgrims still would have stepped onto the *Mayflower*?

2. Tell why you think William Bradford was such a good and long-lasting leader for the Pilgrims.

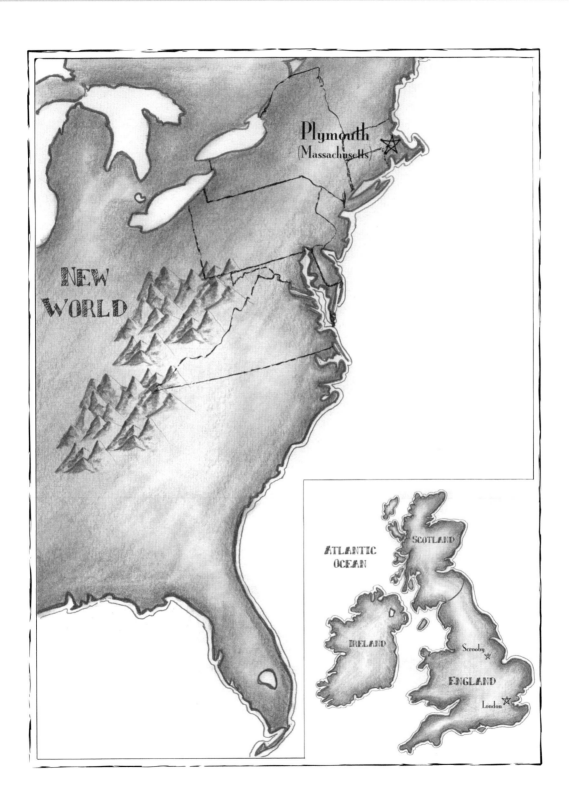

Plymouth
(Massachusetts)

NEW
WORLD

ATLANTIC
OCEAN

SCOTLAND

IRELAND

Scrooby

ENGLAND

London

Timeline Review

Put things in perspective. Place William Bradford's figure on the timeline in the year 1620, which was when he and the Pilgrims set sail for the New World. Look at the other events before, during, and after this year.

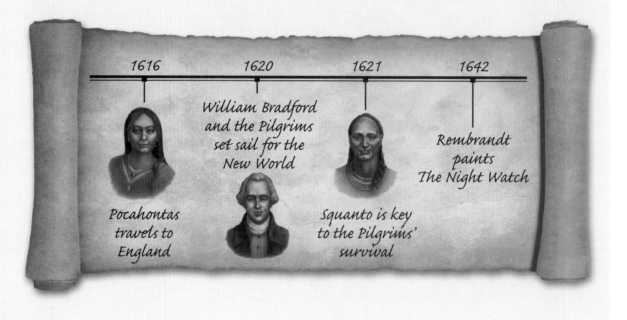

Activity

William Bradford was part of a group known as the Separatists. That means they did many things differently from the people around them. Make a list of the things you do the same as other people in your neighborhood, and another list of the things you do differently. Are you a separatist in your neighborhood?

Wordscramble

Here is a list of scrambled words that relate to the profile you read about William Bradford. Unscramble the letters and write the words correctly.

1. woyrlaeMf _____
2. ufgeer _____
3. liirgpsm _____
4. upeospr _____
5. aptrSeisast _____

6. eonlb _____
7. iveelsreb _____
8. eovgornr _____
9. rslpiadhee _____
10. eisevrc _____

True or False

After reading the profile about William Bradford, decide whether the following statements are true or false.

1. _____ The Pilgrims wanted to be separate from the Church of England.

2. _____ King James was kind to people who disagreed with him.

3. _____ The Pilgrims lived in several large rooms as they crossed the ocean to America.

4. _____ The Mayflower Compact was a small place on the ship where people went to pray.

5. _____ The Pilgrims arrived in America during the winter.

Cloze

After reading the profile, try to fill in the blanks with words that make sense about William Bradford. When you are finished, look at the story to find the words that were used in the passage.

These were not the kind of people to _____ easily, but Bradford _____ out even among such _____ believers. It's easy to see that he was very _____, and was able to see past _____ to the rewards ahead. The noble William Bradford was a _____ with a strong _____ for the 'saints,' as they called themselves. As a matter of fact, he played an important part in every major _____ they made.

William Bradford Word Search

```
W D W U N S E P A R A T I S T S Z L E
J D C H Q N E K T N V G Y D L Z A O Y
Z M G O V E R N O R D L D P P H W B J
O D L E A D E R S H I P U K P Q N D K
B P J R O U S D F O L F J Y H Q U T P
R C B R H D U M A Y F L O W E R S F U
U B C O P B F U G W I Z O B R K I Z R
Y U F L I W K P F N O B L E F L L H P
V V J W L Q M V K P K G V A E J A P O
T V X D G M E J W A A J L Z L U O K S
R G K Z R S E R V I C E J P E S B R E
S G I P I M R J S P P N Z T Y C B O I
B J W V M B E L I E V E R S K Y X R N
V J J E S D A U I R P R E F U G E I M
E H Q P V I S O Y Y Q Y M O Y R K C X
```

Word Bank

Mayflower

refuge

Pilgrims

purpose

Separatists

noble

believers

governor

leadership

service

William Bradford Crossword

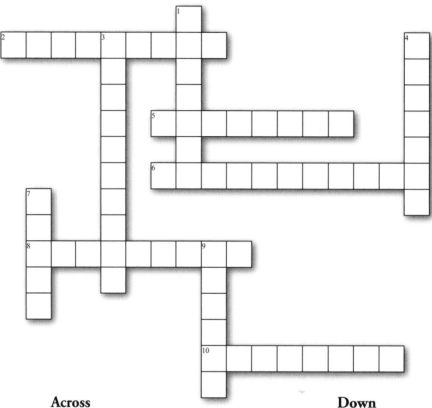

Across

2. Name of the ship that brought the Pilgrims to the New World

5. The group of people who traveled to the New World with William Bradford were known by this name

6. Name of the group of people who wanted to separate from the Church of England

8. What people who strongly believe in something are called

10. William Bradford was elected to this position when John Carver died

Down

1. The second character quality that helped the Pilgrims agree on Bradford's election as governor

3. This was one of the character qualities that kept any of the Pilgrims from objecting to Bradford's election as governor

4. Even parting with loved ones could not turn the Pilgrims away from this

7. A word used to describe William Bradford that indicates he was a man of strong character

9. Word that means a safe place, and one of the things the Pilgrims hoped to find in the New World

Squanto

There have been many different accounts of the life of Squanto, or Tisquantum, which was his original name. Squanto was a Native American who was born around the 1590's. His home was in America, almost at the exact spot where the Plymouth Pilgrims eventually landed. Squanto lived during an age of exploration. This was a time when many people of the world wanted freedom from the lives and unjust governments they had been born into.

Some people believe that Squanto was a deceptive and selfish person; others think he was a man of great honor. We will never have the chance to know Squanto's true nature, but from the main events of his life we can get an idea about his character. There is one thing we do know however: if it wasn't for Squanto's help, the Pilgrims might not have lived through their second winter in the New World.

Squanto was born in a place called Patuxet, which later became known as Plymouth. When he was still a young boy, he met his first white man. Soon there were many white men who were sent to the New World to see what natural resources could be found and to explore the surrounding areas. These men came from a far off place, carrying shiny trinkets, and they interested Squanto very much. The captain of the voyage that brought them, George Weymouth, invited Squanto to travel back to England on his ship. Squanto was excited to go, and left his family and everything that was familiar to him. He wanted adventure, and probably got more than he bargained for!

During his time with the Englishmen, Squanto learned their language and customs. Try to imagine the adventures he must have had! It would have been interesting to see the look on his face when he arrived in England for the first time. How hard it must have been for him to adjust to such a modern lifestyle.

Years later, John Smith was captain of one of a pair of ships sailing from England to the New World. Squanto's chance to return home had finally come. Although he had to work while sailing with John Smith, Smith did take Squanto home during the journey.

While Smith was exploring the eastern coast of America, he arrived in the region where Squanto was born. It had been nearly ten years since Squanto had seen his home and his family, and he was surely very eager to get back. After Smith landed at Plymouth, he left Squanto there and headed northeast to carry on with his business. But before Squanto got a chance to see his home, Thomas Hunt (captain of the second ship that had sailed with them) kidnapped him along with several other Patuxet Indians. He took the captives to Malaga, Spain to sell them as slaves. Fortunately, a group of monks from a local monastery discovered what Captain Hunt was doing and took the remaining Indians from him. Squanto stayed with the monks for about a year, and then he went back to England. He did not return to his birthplace in America until 1619, when he traveled back to the New World with Captain Thomas Dermer.

For Squanto however, it was no longer home. His family was gone, his town was gone, and all that he remembered of home was lost. He learned that since his last visit, every member of the Patuxet tribe had died of a horrible disease. It is unknown exactly what sickness the Patuxet Indians died from, but some historians believe that it was smallpox. Because of Squanto's great loss he decided to stay with Captain Dermer for a time, and they explored the coast together. On many outings, Squanto acted as interpreter for the explorers. They visited the Pokanoket country where a great chief, Sachem Massasoit, lived. Squanto must have really liked the Pokanokets, because after his visit he chose to stay with them.

After Captain Dermer left Squanto at his new home he continued with his explorations. On one of his journeys, the captain was captured by the Nauset Indians. When Squanto heard about his captured friend, he came to his aid as quickly as possible. Squanto bargained for Captain Dermer's safe release. He did not come to the captain's aid for any profit of his own, but because he knew he could help.

Squanto stayed with Massasoit and the Pokanokets for about a year. Then one day, his friend Samoset told him of a ship that was full of English men and women. He took Squanto to visit the colonists, because Samoset knew that his friend could speak their language. He also spoke English, but not as well as Squanto. After Squanto's first visit with the Pilgrims that day, he never left them.

Squanto helped the English have peace with Massasoit and his tribe. The Indians and the Pilgrims kept that peace in the region for fifty years. The Pilgrims were having great difficulty growing enough crops to feed their entire colony, and Squanto showed them how to fertilize the soil so that their crops could grow well. He taught them the best places to fish and hunt, how to catch eels, and which berries were good to eat. Whenever the Pilgrims traveled, Squanto acted as their interpreter and guide. During his time in the colony, he lived with Governor William Bradford. Bradford and Squanto had great respect for each other. After Squanto's death, Bradford said that he was "a special instrument sent by God for their good, beyond their expectation."

Although Squanto served the Pilgrims for only two years, that time is his greatest legacy. He died from a fever with William Bradford by his side while acting as interpreter on one of their many voyages. The Pilgrims suffered a great loss that day, but they would always remember what their friend Squanto had done for them, and they remained forever grateful.

Discussion

1. Do you think Squanto liked the easier way of life in England, or do you think he might have longed for home?

2. Many unexpected things happened to Squanto, and he endured many trials. After reading this profile, tell what you admire most about him.

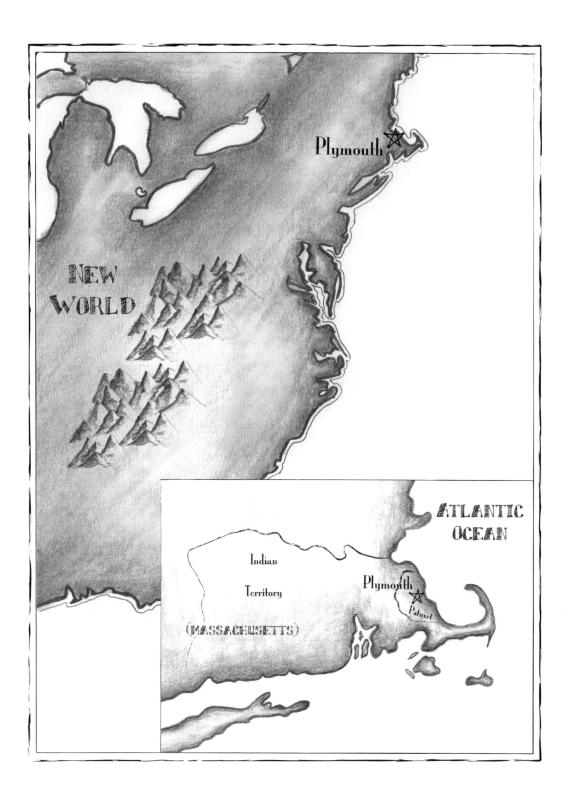

Timeline Review

Put things in perspective. Place Squanto's figure on the timeline in the year 1621, which was when he was key to the Pilgrims' survival in the New World. Look at the other events before, during and after this year.

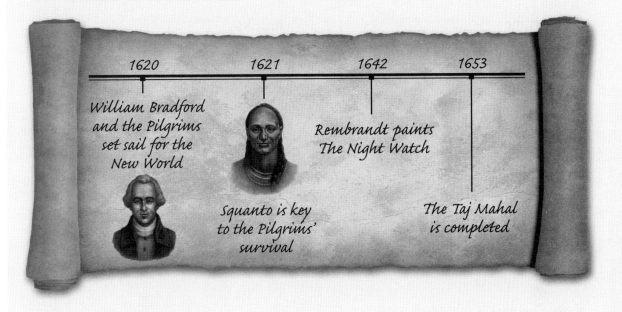

1620 — William Bradford and the Pilgrims set sail for the New World

1621 — Squanto is key to the Pilgrims' survival

1642 — Rembrandt paints The Night Watch

1653 — The Taj Mahal is completed

Activity

Pretend you are going on a long journey to a new place to live. Make a list of things you would take with you to remind you of home. Now look at your list and choose the three most important things to you and tell why.

Wordscramble

Here is a list of scrambled words that relate to the profile you read about Squanto. Unscramble the letters and write the words correctly.

1. nqaisuTumt _____
2. crcatrahe _____
3. uePaxtt _____
4. aterdenvu _____
5. ryueojn _____

6. aeslvs _____
7. nmoks _____
8. aosllpmx _____
9. nrerepttire _____
10. eaecp _____

Sequencing

After reading the profile about Squanto, put the following events in order. Use the numbers 1–5.

A. _____ Many white men came to the New World to find natural resources and explore.

B. _____ Squanto was born in Patuxet.

C. _____ Captain Weymouth invited Squanto to travel to England.

D. _____ Squanto was very interested in the men who came from far away.

E. _____ Squanto left his family and everything that was familiar to him.

Cloze

After reading the profile, try to fill in the blanks with words that make sense about Squanto. When you are finished, look at the story to find the words that were used in the passage.

Squanto helped the English have _____ with Massasoit and his tribe. The Indians and the Pilgrims kept that peace in the region for fifty years. The Pilgrims were having great difficulty growing enough crops to feed their entire colony, and Squanto showed them how to _____ the soil so that their crops could grow well. He taught them the best places to fish and hunt, how to catch eels, and which berries were good to eat. Whenever the Pilgrims traveled, Squanto acted as their _____ and _____ . During his time in the colony, he lived with Governor William Bradford. Bradford and Squanto had great _____ for each other. After Squanto's death, Bradford said that he was "a special instrument sent by _____ for their good, beyond their expectation."

Squanto Word Search

```
P G V K D Q U I S M A L L P O X N F G
E X U J L Z Q N R G C Y J P X N H G V
P J E J M D S T S Y B I Q T Q Z C T E
E O E B H Q Y E E R T O Q R J H H K
A D V E N T U R E S L A V E S T H Q P
C U M P B C E P A L L Q J W Y A V S E
E S U A X G A R E C Z P O A O I M B K
C D W T B L G E T I S Q U A N T U M N
Z T F U O E T T W R B U R Y X I R T X
T K P X E K Q E M G M O N K S V O N T
J V P E V E O R Z I Z V E Z D O G K N
E I E T G I Z G X G M X Y X J V J F A
B T V A Q R H P F N Y O B B F B Q I J
Y X Q P T R I N Y C E F Y T Z F Z R I
V D T Y Y C H A R A C T E R I P J U U
```

Word Bank

Tisquantum
character
Patuxet
adventure
journey

slaves
monks
smallpox
interpreter
peace

Squanto Crossword

Across

1. Place where Squanto was born
4. One of the jobs that Squanto did for the Pilgrims
7. Squanto and his friends were kidnapped and taken to Spain to be sold as these
9. Word that means a long trip
10. A word that refers to a person's true nature

Down

2. Something Squanto wanted that caused him to leave home and sail to England
3. The group of people from a monastery who rescued Squanto from the slave market
5. The thing that Squanto helped the Pilgrims have with Massasoit and his tribe
6. Squanto's original name
8. The disease that many people believe killed Squanto's tribe

Benjamin Franklin

Benjamin Franklin was a man who, instead of thinking about ways he could become famous or make his fortune, tried to think of ways he could help the community around him. He was the youngest in a family with seventeen children. Surely that was one way that he learned the importance of helping and serving others.

Franklin believed in making the most of life, and time, and he did just that. He was, among many other things, a scientist and inventor. One of his most famous inventions was a heat-efficient stove, called the Franklin Stove, which helped people keep their homes warm during the cold winter months. Although he could have taken out a patent on the stove's design and made a lot of money, he didn't because wealth wasn't important to him. He also invented the lightning rod, which is a metal rod placed on top of a structure. During thunderstorms lightning is attracted to the rod, allowing strikes to be channeled harmlessly into the ground without damaging anything. Franklin did not take out a patent for this invention either, and instead published instructions on how to build the lightning rod so that everyone could use and benefit from it.

He was always interested in finding a better way. Many people talk about finding better ways, but never actually try to change or improve anything. However, if Ben had a good idea he could be counted on to do everything in his power to bring it about. While living in Philadelphia, he helped establish that city's first library, first fire department, and first hospital. Ben also started a newspaper there called the *Pennsylvania Gazette*. Through it he was able to print his thoughts and strong political opinions. He managed to make them interesting and fun to read by designing the very first political cartoons, and writing articles filled with humor and wisdom. For over twenty-five years his *Poor Richard's Almanack* was a popular publication in the American Colonies. It was especially known for Franklin's clever observations and proverbs found on the unused squares of the calendar pages. When Franklin became Deputy Postmaster General of America he was put in charge of all the mail in the northern colonies. Under his leadership the delivery of mail became much faster and better, more people began to write letters to each other. As a result the colonies didn't seem so far apart anymore.

Even though he accomplished much during his life, many believe that Ben's most important contributions happened during the Revolutionary War. This war against England's control over the New World lasted eight years. By its end the United States had been established, and America had finally won freedom. However, at the end of the second year of war America was not doing well. Ben Franklin was given the very important mission of going to France and asking for help. Fortunately, the French respected Ben very much and agreed to come to the aid of the colonies. This gave America the strength and hope that they needed to fight the British soldiers. Later, he was one of the five men who wrote the United States Constitution.

When Benjamin Franklin died in the year 1790, he was 84 years old. Twenty thousand people attended his funeral. The fact that such a large number of people came to honor his life, speaks much louder than words ever could about this man's contributions and achievements.

Discussion

1. Benjamin Franklin was the first person to express his political views by using cartoon drawings. With your parent's help, look in a newspaper or magazine for some political cartoons. Pick one and talk with your parent about what the cartoonist is saying in his drawing. Ask your parent if he or she agrees with the cartoon. Why or why not? Do you agree with your parent?

2. Imagine that you have sixteen older brothers and sisters. Talk with your parent about how this might affect your life.

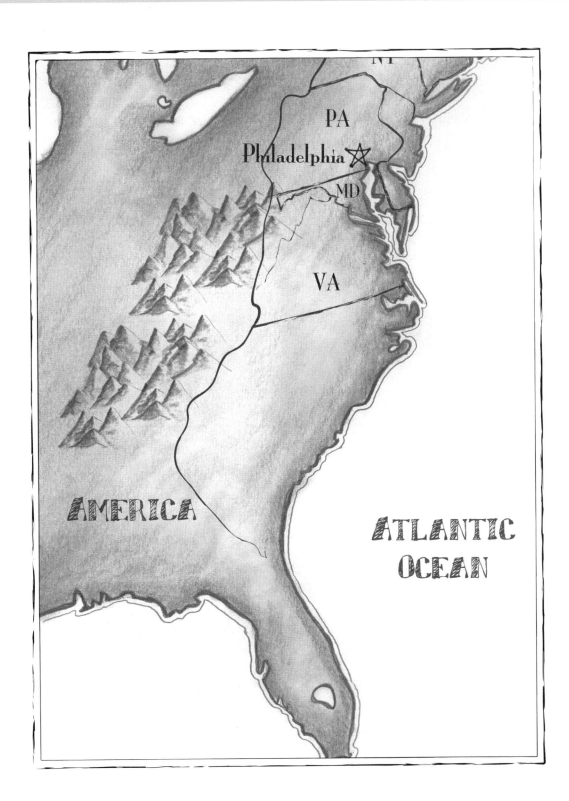

Timeline Review

Put things in perspective. Place Benjamin Franklin's figure on the timeline in the year 1732, which was when he first published *Poor Richard's Almanack.* Look at the other events before, during, and after this year.

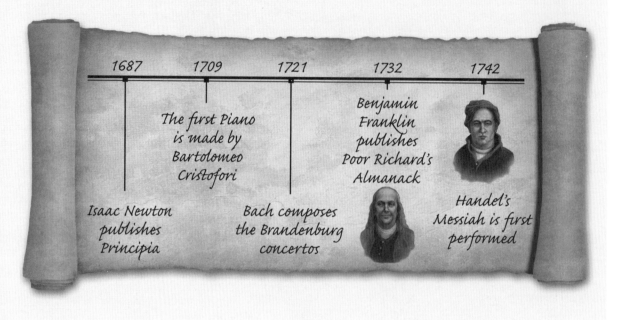

1687   1709   1721   1732   1742

The first Piano is made by Bartolomeo Cristofori

Benjamin Franklin publishes Poor Richard's Almanack

Isaac Newton publishes Principia

Bach composes the Brandenburg concertos

Handel's Messiah is first performed

Activity

Ben Franklin emphasized the importance of communication. As the first Postmaster General, he encouraged all Americans to exchange news, opinions, business matters, and affairs of government.

Read about the U.S. Postal Service. How did the postal service start? How has it changed over the years? What did you learn that surprised you? Write a friendly letter to a family member or friend. With your parent's permission, mail the letter. Contact the person you mailed the letter to and find out how long it took to receive it.

Wordscramble

Here is a list of scrambled words that relate to the profile you read about Benjamin Franklin. Unscramble the letters and write the words correctly.

1. soumaf _____
2. seinsittc _____
3. tervoinn _____
4. aptetn _____
5. ighlgtinn _____

6. irayblr _____
7. epsarpwne _____
8. deerihlaps _____
9. ettrles _____
10. cFnear _____

Sequencing

After reading Benjamin Franklin's profile, put the following events in order. Use the numbers 1–5.

A. _____ He helped write the United States Constitution.

B. _____ He was sent to France to ask for help during the Revolutionary War.

C. _____ He invented the Franklin Stove.

D. _____ He helped establish Philadelphia's first library.

E. _____ He became Deputy Postmaster General.

Cloze

After reading the profile, try to fill in the blanks with words that make sense about Benjamin Franklin. When you are finished, look at the story to find the words that were used in the passage.

Even though he accomplished much during his life, many believe that Ben's most important _____ happened during the Revolutionary War. This war against England's _____ over the New World lasted _____ years, but by its end the United States had been established, and America had finally won freedom. However, at the end of the second year of war America was not doing well. Ben Franklin was given the very important _____ of going to France and asking for _____. Fortunately, the French _____ Ben very much and agreed to come to the aid of the _____. This gave America the strength and _____ that they needed to fight the British soldiers. Later, he was one of the five men who wrote the United States Constitution.

Benjamin Franklin Word Search

```
J E B I S V K A I G N K X M Q Q U E J
L I G H T N I N G U X U C K C P Q E P
H L N G T Z Q M U B T N R N B A J T T
G G H I L A H Z O Y J J P F V T R Y S
J Q L E A D E R S H I P K A M E U X H
A N L A S Y Z K V T Z K M M V N M B N
L Y Q U C T L F G A H I W O B T Y O E
E I Q I I T B O K L F N Z U B I G L W
T L W H E L Y X D I L V I S J L I C S
T Z T I N V N X B S E J I P Y F A P
E M X J T Q A G X R F N Q O T E G A R
R Z V Y I B W M T A I T N N O T T P
S U I M S Q Z M A R N O X R J I F T E
G A L S T J X J E Y F R A N C E N N R
I N O I L D V N I E O H I F X O T R X
```

Word Bank

famous
scientist
inventor
patent
lightning

library
newspaper
leadership
letters
France

Benjamin Franklin Crossword

Across

4. Ben started one of these and called it the *Pennsylvania Gazette*

6. While Ben was Deputy Postmaster General, people began to write more of these to each other

8. A person who explores things in nature and science

9. What a person is called when he comes up with new ideas for making or doing things

10. A place where books are kept

Down

1. Because of this, the delivery of mail when Ben was in charge became much faster and better

2. Country where Ben was sent to ask for help during the Revolutionary War

3. Another word for being very well-known

5. A legal document that keeps other people from copying an invention Ben refused to get one for his stove

7. During thunderstorms, this is attracted to the special rod that Ben invented

George Frideric Handel

It is said that it took Handel only twenty-four days to create one of the world's best-known musical masterpieces, the *Messiah*. This beautiful composition debuted on a very special Easter morning in 1742, when Handel was 57 years old. He showed us that when a person is inspired and passionate, great works can be done in a short time. Handel had a reputation for needing little time to compose his works.

He was born in Germany in the same year as Johann Sebastian Bach, 1685. They lived only fifty miles from each other, yet never met. Handel's father expected him to become a lawyer, but as fate would have it he never followed that path. His musical career began as a boy at the age of seven when he taught himself to play the harpsichord, which is a primitive version of the piano. As Handel grew he became assistant organist at his home church while continuing to learn new instruments, and soon he was arranging the choral compositions every Sunday. Handel's talent was clearly undeniable, and as he persisted his career flourished.

To compose a masterpiece, a musician must have a vast knowledge of many instruments and be a master of several, which Handel was. Because he began composing music at the age of nine, one can't help but wonder where his inspiration came from. Did he hear the music in his head and then write it all down in a flurry of notes? Or did the ideas come to him as he played an instrument? It is speculated that Handel wrote *Messiah* in a garden temple; perhaps he was inspired by its beauty. The most famous movement of *Messiah* is the "Hallelujah Chorus." In many places around the world it is a tradition to stand during this movement. King George II supposedly started this tradition at one of the earlier performances of *Messiah*. Legend says that the King was so moved by the music that he rose during its most climactic sequence. Because of royal etiquette at that time, every other person in the audience followed his lead, and thus began a tradition that has lasted through the centuries. Handel performed *Messiah* countless times throughout the course of his life. Each time he customized the performance to fit the orchestra or singers that were used.

Among Handel's greatest achievements was writing four anthems for the coronation ceremony of King George II. He was commissioned to do this by King George himself. One of these anthems is called "Zadok the Priest," and it has been performed at every British coronation ceremony since then. If only Handel had known at the time he was composing "Zadok the Priest" that he was adding to the history and tradition of a nation.

On April 6, 1759 in London, England Handel gave his very last performance; he was 74 years old. The piece he performed was *Messiah*, and he died only eight days later. His death occurred the day before Easter, the day before the 18th anniversary of *Messiah's* very first performance. This great composer was honored by a burial at Westminster Abbey along with the past Kings and Queens of England, as well as the likes of Sir Isaac Newton and Charles Dickens. Beethoven once said that he saw Handel as the greatest composer who ever lived, and there are many who agree with him.

Discussion

1. It was not unusual for great composers in the past to work for the church or for the king or queen of a country. It was considered the highest compliment that could be made to a composer's music. Do you think that is still true today? What do you think makes a composer great by today's standards? Do you think today's standards are a good measure of greatness?

2. King George stood to his feet during the first performance of the "Hallelujah Chorus." It is said that this was his response to the music. After listening to the "Hallelujah Chorus" yourself, do you think King George was right to stand? How does the music make you feel? Have you ever heard music that made you want to move? Tell about it.

Timeline Review

Put things in perspective. Place Handel's figure on the timeline in the year 1742 which was when his famous *Messiah* was first performed. Look at the other events before, during, and after this year.

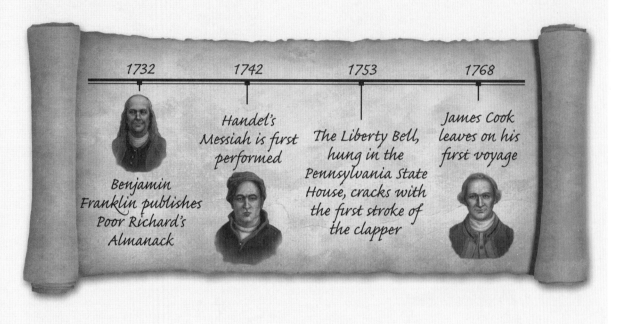

Activity

Listen to the "Hallelujah Chorus" from Handel's *Messiah*. Try to picture King George becoming so moved by the music that he stood. If possible, listen to other works by Handel, such as "Water Music." How do they compare?

Wordscramble

Here is a list of scrambled words that relate to the profile you read about George Frideric Handel. Unscramble the letters and write the words correctly.

1. Hdanle _____

2. iasehMs _____

3. hBac _____

4. shiahcpordr _____

5. sraecmieept _____

6. nnariioipst _____

7. lahelHaulj roCush _____

8. nigK orGeeg _____

9. ocinotrano _____

10. ospercmo _____

True or False

After reading his profile, decide whether each of the following statements about George Frideric Handel is true or false.

1. _____ Handel's music was played for kings.

2. _____ Beethoven did not think Handel was a great composer.

3. _____ Handel was musically talented as a child.

4. _____ Today it is still a tradition to stand during performances of the "Hallelujah Chorus."

5. _____ Handel's music is no longer used when crowning a king or queen in England.

Cloze

After reading the profile, try to fill in the blanks with words that make sense about George Frideric Handel. When you are finished, look at the story to find the words that were used in the passage.

On April 6, 1759 in _____, England, _____ gave his very last performance; he was 74 years old. The piece he performed was _____, and he died only eight days later. His death occurred the day before _____, the day before the 18th anniversary of *Messiah's* very first performance. This great composer was honored by a burial at _____ Abbey along with the past Kings and Queens of England, as well as the likes of Sir Isaac Newton and Charles Dickens. _____ once said that he saw Handel as the _____ composer who ever lived, and there are many who agree with him.

George Frideric Handel Word Search

```
G D R W C K H A R P S I C H O R D M E
Q M D Y F O B F O T T T J I A I I E Y
G T T G X V S T L Y R X C Y K N S S O
O D O H X Y Q Q Q V F G B A I P C S W
W A Y I Z U S U F K K I H J N U O I C
S W D Y D R F S Y H Y D N F G Z R A E
W I N S P I R A T I O N D T G X O H J
K Q M A S T E R P I E C E U E E N W O
F R H A N D E L K P K H O T O S A T S
N F I U P L T R X R G R T D R R T J C
X L J D Y N B A C H X Q X D G N I W T
Y K F D M R E P C O M P O S E R O N O
A O K R F S O Z G J K S Y C B R N E B
S H W L Z O O S B E S U X K S F N A Y
E H A L L E L U J A H C H O R U S Z D
```

Word Bank

Handel
Messiah
Bach
harpsichord
masterpiece

inspiration
Hallelujah Chorus
King George
coronation
composer

George Frideric Handel Crossword

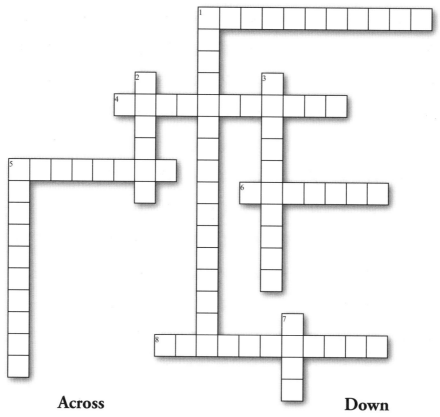

Across

1. The first musical instrument that Handel learned to play

4. A musician must have a vast knowledge of many instruments to compose one of these

5. This is what a person who writes music is called

6. The musical composition that contains the "Hallelujah Chorus"

8. Since Handel began composing music so young, it is hard to imagine where he got this

Down

1. It is tradition to stand when this piece of music is performed

2. Beethoven considered this man the greatest composer who ever lived

3. Handel was commissioned to write music for this person's coronation ceremony

5. This is a crowning ceremony for a king or queen

7. The name of another great composer who was born in the same year and only 50 miles from Handel

James Cook

There have been many people throughout history who devoted their lives to the sea. Perhaps they were entranced by its beauty. The ocean is both a beautiful and a terrifying entity, not to be trifled with. Some days a person can look out on a crisp morning and see a magnificent view of the ocean waters calmly sweeping the sand back and forth. The sun shines down on the sparkling water, and the soft melody of the waves fills the senses. There are other days however, in which the ocean can seem relentless and angry. Why then do some people devote their lives to such an untrustworthy companion? Most people will probably never understand.

No doubt a person must be very brave to put his life into the hands of the sea, and that is just what James Cook was. Not only was he fearless, intelligent, and determined, but Cook also had a deep love for the ocean. He knew as soon as he saw her that his career would be on the open seas. He worked long and hard to be able to command his own ship. With no previous background, he learned as much as he could about the subjects necessary for that to happen -- math, navigation, and astronomy.

James joined the merchant navy as a teenager, and then went on to the Royal Navy. There, his mapping abilities made him a vital asset to England during the Seven Years' War. This conflict officially began when England declared war against France in 1756, and it eventually involved all of the major powers in Europe. James' mapping skills allowed his leader, General Wolfe, to make a surprise attack during an important battle. After this, his reputation preceded him. A good map of the area about to be attacked allowed for in-depth planning and precise tactics, both very necessary in war.

Having found recognition for his surveying and mapping skills, James was recruited by the Royal Society to explore and claim the lands he found for England. The society knew that they had found the person they needed to explore in England's name. They needed a superior Captain during this critical time in history when land was being discovered and taken by countries around the world. For his part, James Cook wanted to sail farther than any man had gone before. So he did. He went farther south than any other explorer had when he sailed fearlessly into the treacherous waters of the Antarctic Circle. He brought back new knowledge of the Pacific Ocean through his various travels, and made an even bigger name for himself when he created the first large-scale, precise map of the coast of Newfoundland. Cook spent many years dedicated to discovering new lands and paths. He became the first European to encounter and chart the eastern coastline of Australia, the first to come across the Hawaiian Islands, and the first to sail all the way around New Zealand.

In addition, Captain Cook always made a point to take care of his crew. He made them bathe every day, wash their belongings, exercise, and he kept fresh fruits and vegetables on board for the men as much as possible. Scurvy, caused by lack of Vitamin C, was a very common disease among sailors. Cook's men never contracted this disease due to their Captain's strict policies. Although it cost more money to maintain a better lifestyle and diet on board his ship, Cook was determined to keep his men healthy.

James Cook sailed around the world twice, and made many discoveries. Following his very first voyage, he was promoted from Master to Commander. After his second voyage he progressed from Commander to Captain. Even though James started his career as an apprentice on a coal carrying boat in the merchant navy, from there he was able to shape a very important place in history. Throughout his life he made his English homeland and his family very proud. Some have even said that James Cook was one of the world's greatest explorers.

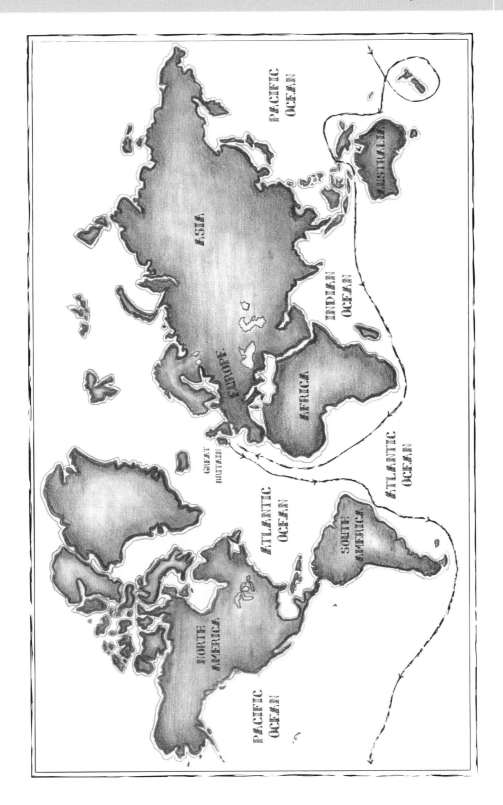

Discussion

1. Captain Cook was given many promotions as a ship's captain. Why do you think this happened? Find at least three reasons in the profile for Captain Cook's success.

2. Many sailors during Captain Cook's time were not very healthy. What did he do to help take care of his men? How do you think this contributed to his success as a captain?

Timeline Review

Put things in perspective. Place James Cook's figure on the timeline in the year 1768, which was when he left on his first voyage. Look at the other events before, during, and after this year.

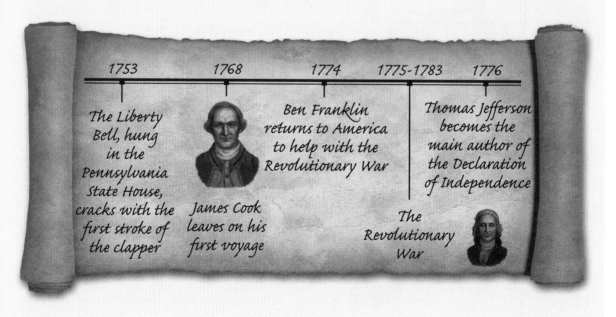

1753 — The Liberty Bell, hung in the Pennsylvania State House, cracks with the first stroke of the clapper

1768 — James Cook leaves on his first voyage

1774 — Ben Franklin returns to America to help with the Revolutionary War

1775-1783 — The Revolutionary War

1776 — Thomas Jefferson becomes the main author of the Declaration of Independence

Activity

Look at a globe and find the places mentioned in Captain Cook's profile. What do these places have in common? How are they different? What hemisphere, or section of the globe, are they in? Tell what you know about each place. Choose one place to learn more about.

Wordscramble

Here is a list of scrambled words that relate to the profile you read about James Cook. Unscramble the letters and write the words correctly.

1. toiiaavnng _____

2. amyoornst _____

3. pmaingp _____

4. atnrccAit _____

5. lAtaaursi _____

6. patnaCi okoC _____

7. cyrvus _____

8. rMaets _____

9. erCmoandm _____

10. yaNv _____

Cloze

After reading the profile, try to fill in the blanks with words that make sense about James Cook. When you are finished, look at the story to find the words that were used in the passage.

Having found _____ for his _____ and mapping skills, James was recruited by the Royal Society to explore and claim the lands he found for _____. The society knew that they had found the person they needed to _____ in England's name. They needed a _____ Captain during this critical time in history when land was being _____ and taken by countries around the world. For his part, James Cook wanted to sail _____ than any man had gone before. So he did. He went farther south than any other explorer had when he sailed fearlessly into the treacherous waters of the _____ Circle. He brought back new knowledge of the _____ Ocean through his various travels, and made an even bigger name for himself when he created the first large-scale, precise map of the coast of _____. James spent many years dedicated to discovering new lands and paths. He became the first _____ to encounter and chart the eastern coastline of Australia, the first to come across the _____ Islands, and the first to sail all the way around New Zealand.

Sequencing

Put the following places in the order that they are mentioned in Captain Cook's profile. Use numbers 1–5.

A. _____ Newfoundland

B. _____ Australia

C. _____ Antarctic Circle

D. _____ Hawaiian Islands

E. _____ New Zealand

James Cook Word Search

```
R I S C U R V Y T R N U E G X C P Q T
Q F V A U W G W B X S L C V L C H E U
C O M M A N D E R D X Y M P F A H N B
G P A N T A R C T I C J M L V P F A F
O E S L C Y B K A A U N D E T Q V H
A C T L F V J A U S T R A L I A T Y L
N P E A D F Q C R T Y U V R Y I D U P
J Q R E G P A M I R A N I T Y N B V M
Z K X L X O R S Y O V L G R H C Q U G
J E L P K R P T Q N T Q A G U O O S H
K L X X Q R I E V O X W T Y H O H I C
J P M A P P I N G M S G I Z Q K W N S
B J L X U Z I T N Y H P O L O R V W V
O P D J K Z B S N S N N Z V E Q X W
N T R F H O R W N F U F U X V K M J E
```

Word Bank

Antarctic

Australia

Captain Cook

Commander

Master

astronomy

mapping

navigation

navy

scurvy

James Cook Crossword

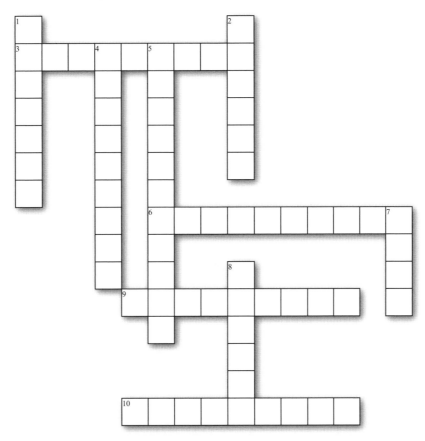

Across

3. Captain Cook sailed farther south than any other explorer had when he entered the treacherous waters near this continent

6. One of the subjects James Cook learned to prepare him for his career

9. Following his first voyage, James was promoted to this rank

10. James Cook was the first European to chart the eastern coastline of this continent

Down

1. The part of Cook's work that was a vital asset to England during the Seven Years War

2. A disease caused by the lack of Vitamin C

4. The scientific study of the universe that helped James Cook prepare for his future

5. This explorer always made it a point to take care of his crew

7. James began his career on the sea in the merchant branch of this service

8. During James Cook's first voyage, this was his rank

Thomas Jefferson

America needed freedom! England, which governed most of the New World, had become much too greedy and was taking advantage of the colonies. Taxes had increased steadily over the years, and most Americans had become convinced that England was only interested in their hard-earned money. Thomas Jefferson was born into this political climate in 1743, so it's not surprising that as a young man he adopted freedom as his life's mission.

In 1776, at the age of 33, Jefferson became the main author of the Declaration of Independence. This important document stated that America was a new, free country, no longer subject to its English oppressors. It listed reasons why freedom was necessary and laid a foundation for the new government that would soon be established. The following passage from the Declaration was written with wisdom that has stood for over 200 years:

"We hold these truths to be self-evident, that all men are created equal, that they are endowed by their Creator with certain unalienable Rights, that among these are Life, Liberty and the pursuit of Happiness.--That to secure these rights, Governments are instituted among Men, deriving their just powers from the consent of the governed. . ."

In 1779, in the midst of the Revolutionary War, Thomas Jefferson became governor of his home state of Virginia. Then, a few years later he accepted the position of the United States' representative to France, where he served for 5 years. When George Washington became President in 1789, he appointed Jefferson his Secretary of State. Three years after resigning from that office, Jefferson became a reluctant presidential candidate and was quite surprised when he came within three votes of winning the election. He lost to John Adams but because he was the runner-up, under the system then in effect, he became Vice President. Jefferson was troubled by things he saw in the government that he felt were threats to America's newly won freedom. So, in the next election he ran for president again, this time more enthusiastically – and he won!

Thomas Jefferson was considered both inspiring and gracious. He became our third president fully aware of the responsibilities of that position, and in his inaugural speech mentioned that he felt ". . . the task is above my talents." This humility, coupled with natural leadership abilities, served him well through two terms as president. Although his decisions were not always popular, he was referred to as "the man of the people."

Jefferson died quietly on July 4, 1826, at his home in Monticello, Virginia. It seems fitting that he died on the day Americans celebrate their freedom -- the anniversary of the day that Congress adopted the Declaration of Independence. Not only that, but 1826 was the 50th anniversary of his famous Declaration. A man of many talents and accomplishments, Thomas Jefferson will always be remembered as the author of American freedom.

Discussion

1. Thomas Jefferson accomplished many things in his life. Among other things he helped write one of the most important documents in United States history, he was a governor, an ambassador, and the third president of our country. When he was a child, do you think he had any idea what his future would hold? Why, or why not? What do you think helped prepare him for the future?

2. Talk with your parent about what you would like to accomplish, or do, or be in the future.

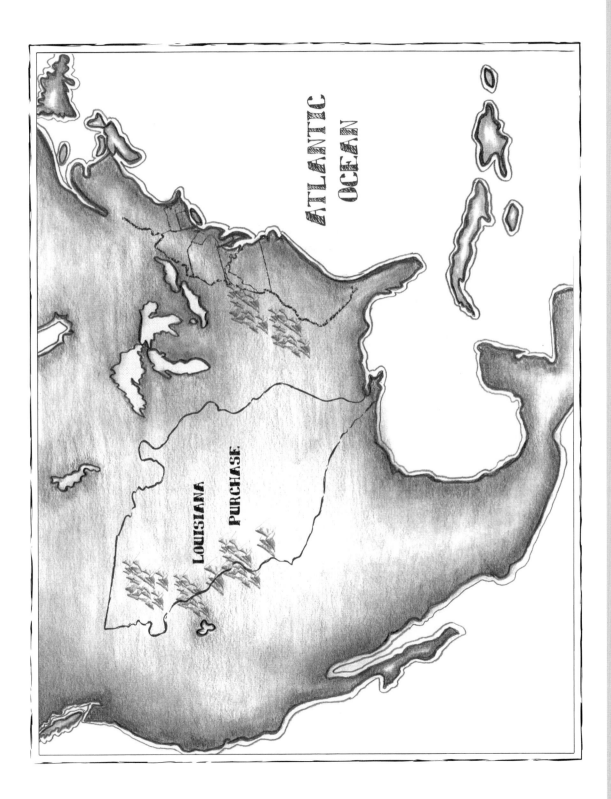

ATLANTIC OCEAN

LOUISIANA PURCHASE

Timeline Review

Put things in perspective. Place Thomas Jefferson's figure on the timeline in the year 1776, which was when he coauthored the Declaration of Independence. Look at the other events before, during, and after this year.

1775-1783 1776 1789

Thomas Jefferson becomes the main author of the Declaration of Independence

The Revolutionary War

Mozart begins writing his Piano Concertos

George Washington becomes the first President of the United States

Activity

Thomas Jefferson designed and built his famous Virginia home, which is called Monticello. Look up pictures and information about Monticello at the library or, with your parent's permission, on the Internet. Then, use a piece of graph paper and design a home that you might like to live in some day. Be sure to include things that you think are important.

One of Thomas Jefferson's most important contributions to the United States was the Louisiana Purchase. Learn about this important purchase. Do you think it was a good decision? Why, or why not?

Wordscramble

Here is a list of scrambled words that relate to the profile you read about Thomas Jefferson. Unscramble the letters and write the words correctly.

1. mossini _____

2. auhrot _____

3. dsmiwo _____

4. vrognoer _____

5. tastnrperievee _____

6. renepitds _____

7. otudlber _____

8. isinnprgi _____

9. tihimylu _____

10. Mtcinelool _____

Sequencing

After reading about Thomas Jefferson, put the following events in the order that they are mentioned in his profile. Use the numbers 1–5.

A. _____ Thomas Jefferson became our third president.

B. _____ Jefferson helped write the Declaration of Independence.

C. _____ He became governor of Virginia.

D. _____ Jefferson adopted freedom as his mission in life.

E. _____ Thomas Jefferson lost an election to John Adams.

Cloze

After reading the profile, try to fill in the blanks with words that make sense about Thomas Jefferson. When you are finished, look at the story to find the words that were used in the passage.

Thomas Jefferson was considered both inspiring and gracious. He became our

_____ president fully aware of the _____ of that position,

and in his inaugural _____ mentioned that he felt ". . . the task is

above my _____." This humility, coupled with natural _____

abilities, served him well through _____ terms as president. Although his

decisions were not always _____, he was referred to as "the man of the

_____."

Thomas Jefferson Word Search

```
M W C R U G G S C C M M E D W G G O X
E M S M D A U T H O R I O H U O S O C
I A B T I P G G U F P S F M Z I T A H
G O V E R N O R M R U S J E Q E R N C
J O E E W U Q L I O T I I T G J O F X
D E Q V X Q P W L Z W O W U Q S U J Y
B W O L W D F R I Z G N V U S W B X G
L I I F B M O N T I C E L L O J L P L
N S D J O B O H Y W H R S J T D E H U
V D O Y C E I N S P I R I N G W D O V
K O O Y V Q X P R E S I D E N T V G X
K M C E R E P R E S E N T A T I V E C
B B K A I I D Y J A V A D H M G Z V M
A W N N O E N N U L Y Y B E R K D I R
V B Y N Y B F R N D G A B B T T I H V
```

Word Bank

mission

author

wisdom

governor

representative

president

troubled

inspiring

humility

Monticello

Thomas Jefferson Crossword

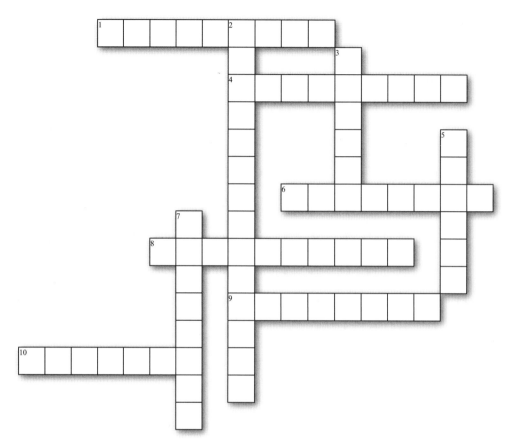

Across

1. Thomas Jefferson was considered to be this, as well as gracious

4. He ran for this office twice, and was elected the second time

6. When someone is humble, they are said to have this quality

8. The place in Virginia where Jefferson died

9. This is how Jefferson felt when he saw things that he felt were threats to America's newly won freedom

10. This is what freedom was to Thomas Jefferson's life

Down

2. Jefferson filled this position for the United States in France

3. A great deal of this went into writing the Declaration of Independence

5. A person who writes something

7. During the Revolutionary War, Jefferson was elected to this office in Virginia

Mozart

Joannes Chrysostomus Wolfgangus Theophilus Mozart. It was quite an elaborate name to live up to! One might expect a man with such a name to do truly great and memorable things. So the question is, did Joannes Chrysostomus Wolfgangus Theophilus Mozart live up to his name? The answer is undeniably yes. As a matter of fact, it would be fair to say that Mozart's extravagant name barely lived up to his incredible life.

In a way, Mozart's love for music seems to have begun even before his birth. His father, Leopold, was a minor composer and had a reputation as an excellent teacher. The very year that Mozart was born his father published a textbook on the violin. Leopold had a great influence on young Mozart's life. He would be Mozart's first teacher, not only of music but also academics.

Mozart was three years old when he first discovered the piano. While his father taught his older sister Nannerl to play, as fate would have it, Mozart found his first love. He began his lifelong career at the age of three by "playing" on the piano. At the age of four Mozart's father began teaching him short piano pieces. Much to Leopold's surprise, Mozart could play the exact piece that his father had played without even one mistake. Likely at this point everyone, including Leopold, knew that the boy had a special gift. When he was five years old Mozart composed his very first piece of music. At that time he was too young to write out the music he played, so his father recorded the notes for him.

As Mozart grew, so did his love for music. Traveling often with his father, Mozart met many famous composers and heard many concerts. Among the composers he was fortunate enough to meet was Johann Christian Bach, who was Johann Sebastian Bach's youngest son. As an adult, Mozart was employed by the Archbishop in his hometown of Salzburg, Austria. He was a beloved composer there, where he gained much experience and self-confidence. During his employment Mozart became interested in violin concertos, and he wrote five at this point in time. These are the only violin concertos he ever wrote, but they remain among the favorites of all time. A violinist must have tremendous talent to keep up with the music. Mozart's piano concertos, however, were his greatest legacy.

Mozart wanted more than hometown fame; he had a much larger vision. Despite his talent, the difficulty of the times made it nearly impossible for Mozart to establish his career in a more prominent place. It wasn't until fairly late in his life that Mozart found the success he was looking for. He moved to Vienna, and at his new home it soon became clear that Mozart was the most excellent pianist that city of musicians could offer. Mozart truly began the movement of piano concertos among composers.

The sad truth for most people is that through their death, their achievements become legendary. This was the case with Mozart. Although popular when he was still alive, through his death his work became invaluable to the history of classical music. Many learned from his ingenious compositions, and many will continue to learn. Mozart's music is timeless. Although he is most appreciated by a certain audience, all generations can value and benefit from his brilliance.

Discussion

1. Mozart's amazing musical ability became obvious at a very young age. How do you think his father encouraged him? Can you think of a talent you have that your parents have encouraged?

2. When people discover a great talent at an early age it can present problems for them. Think about Mozart's life and some of his struggles. What problems could have arisen for him? Talk with your parents about how others may have reacted to him or ways he may have been frustrated. Have you ever experienced any of these problems? If so, how are you and Mozart alike?

Timeline Review

Put things in perspective. Place Mozart's figure on the timeline in the year 1776, which was when he first started writing his Piano Concertos. Look at the other events before, during, and after this year

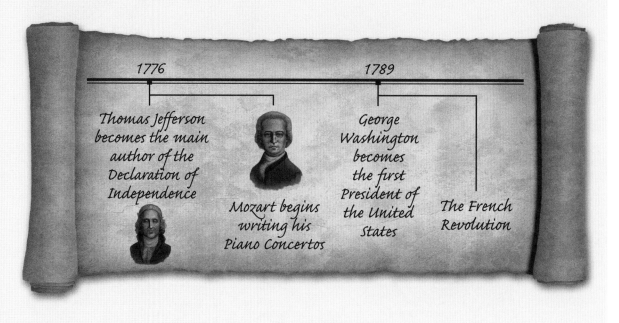

Activity

Listen to several piano concertos composed by Mozart. If possible, listen to other works by Mozart, such as his violin concertos. How do they compare?

Wordscramble

Here is a list of scrambled words that relate to the profile you read about Mozart. Unscramble the letters and write the words correctly.

1. opedloL _____
2. aniop _____
3. aMzotr _____
4. ceoscrtn _____
5. Sbzagrlu _____

6. oivnil _____
7. tltane _____
8. aiuisnmc _____
9. esoprcom _____
10. Vienan _____

Sequencing

Put the following events from Mozart's life in the correct order. Use the numbers 1–5.

A. _____ Mozart moved to Vienna.

B. _____ Mozart discovered the piano.

C. _____ He composed his first piece of music.

D. _____ Mozart wrote five violin concertos.

E. _____ He was employed by the Archbishop in Salzburg.

Cloze

After reading the profile, try to fill in the blanks with words that make sense about Mozart. When you are finished, look at the story to find the words that were used in the passage.

As Mozart grew, so did his love for music. Traveling often with his father,

Mozart met many famous _____ and heard many _____.

Among the composers he was fortunate enough to meet was Johann Christian

_____, who was Johann Sebastian Bach's youngest son. As an

adult, _____ was employed by the Archbishop in his hometown of

_____, Austria. He was a beloved composer there, where he gained

much experience and

self-confidence. During his employment Mozart became interested in

_____ _____ and he wrote five at this point in time. These

are the only violin concertos he ever wrote, but they remain among the favorites

of all time. A violinist must have tremendous talent to keep up with the music.

Mozart's piano concertos, however, were his greatest _____.

Mozart Word Search

```
W M O Z P C Q K O T Z J S T Z M A T M
Q L C K Q O B N S U A F M U O D H U U
D H L C F M C V F Y L H A J Q H K G S
V N Z V L P K I Y A I F T M Y M E W I
S C V H J O O E J A G J S P Z J Q I C
H T Z Q L S Z N J Y P I A N O Z H N I
S R F W I E Z N Z T K V B P N L W T A
A A L N W R S A B B J F M X D N N S N
L L E O P O L D I A S T A L E N T E Q
Z L R Y Q N C Y C O N C E R T S Z T M
B S B Z C M T V I O L I N Z D U H S Q
U E M G J H D F F M Z N Z C N X T B U
R Q F U I A C A R P L G M O Z A R T I
G N Q A H H U B D F M R H U X E F Q L
A U Y G Y O I K H F I P R U E E D G C
```

Word Bank

Leopold

piano

Mozart

concerts

Salzburg

violin

talent

musician

composer

Vienna

Mozart Crossword

Across

1. Another name for musical performances
4. Someone skilled at playing music; there were many of them in Vienna
5. Name of Mozart's father
6. Name of the composer whose greatest legacy is his piano concertos
8. City where Mozart moved and found success as a pianist
9. First musical instrument Mozart learned to play

Down

2. A person who writes music; what Mozart was
3. City in Austria that was Mozart's home town
7. A special gift or ability to do something; violinists had to have a lot of this to play Mozart's concertos
8. Mozart wrote a few concertos for this instrument

Lewis and Clark

Thomas Jefferson grew up in Albemarle, Virginia. He did not know it at the time, but another young man who lived nearby would one day help him achieve a great vision. While growing up, Jefferson became close friends with this neighbor, whose name was Meriwether Lewis. Lewis was treated as a family member by the Jeffersons. Thomas and his old friend, Meriwether Lewis, often talked about exploring the northwestern United States, which at that time was completely unknown.

Many years later, when Thomas Jefferson became our third president, one of the first things he did was ask Lewis to become his personal secretary. In his letter to Lewis, President Jefferson said:

"Your knowledge of the Western country, of the army and of all its interests and relations have rendered it desirable, for public as well as private purposes, that you should be engaged in that office."

He admired Lewis' interest in and knowledge of the West, and believed they would prove important to the United States.

Several years earlier, in Fort Greenville, Ohio, Meriwether Lewis had met a man whose name would eventually be forever linked with his own. After enlisting in the army, Lewis was assigned to a company which was commanded by William Clark. During their time together the two men grew to respect each other and became close friends. Their days as army men taught them many skills that they would later need.

The dreams of exploring the northwestern United States finally became a reality two years after Thomas Jefferson was elected. He named Lewis the head of an operation called the Voyage of Discovery, which most people knew as the Corps of Discovery. The goal of this operation was to explore unknown parts of the country. Lewis was asked to lead an expedition with no maps and no knowledge of what lay ahead. He knew he could not do this alone. He needed someone he could trust, someone with knowledge of the outdoors. He needed William Clark, who wholeheartedly joined the expedition as soon as he was invited.

The Corps of Discovery was hugely successful. They made maps of a part of the country that no one had ever seen before and documented over 300 plants and animals for the very first time. Lewis and Clark reached the Pacific Ocean; they made it to the far side of America and back. The success of their two-year expedition was largely because they worked so well together. From the very beginning, Lewis and Clark shared equal responsibility. Just as they shared responsibilities, they also shared the credit that comes with such an historic expedition. Lewis was actually the first in command of the Corps of Discovery, and William Clark was second. Instead of claiming his glory however, Lewis never told the other men. He referred to Clark as "Captain" and no one ever thought differently.

Lewis and Clark were not average men. They believed in each other, and they believed in their mission. Many times throughout history expeditions like this one have gone horribly wrong, and many lives have been lost in the pursuit of glory and fame. But Lewis and Clark were extraordinary men who led an extraordinary exploration with extraordinary results! They did not seek fame, but they have become famous as the first men to explore the Western United States.

Discussion

1. The Lewis and Clark expedition shows the importance of building relationships. Reread the first four paragraphs of the profile. Tell about the relationship between Thomas Jefferson and Meriwether Lewis. What did President Jefferson think of him? How did their relationship contribute to history?

2. Reread paragraphs 5, 6, 7, and 8. Tell about the relationship between Lewis and Clark. Do you think it mattered to them who was named captain? What does that tell you about their friendship?

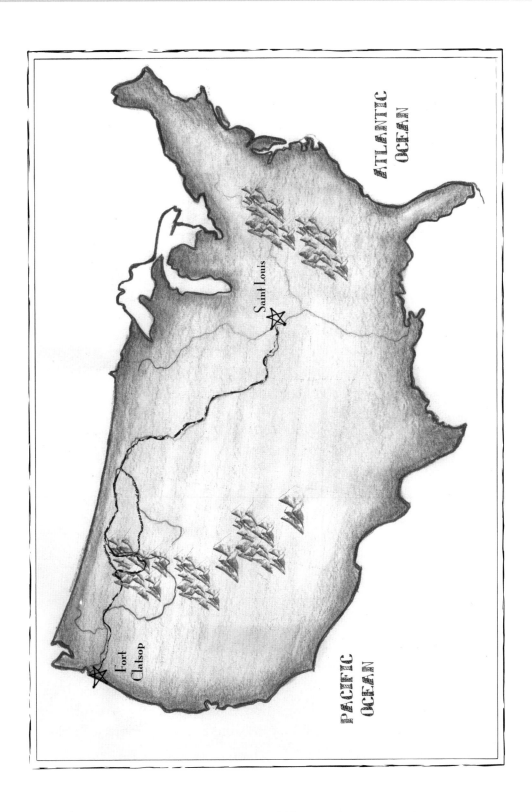

ATLANTIC OCEAN

Saint Louis

Fort Clatsop

PACIFIC OCEAN

Timeline Review

Put things in perspective. Place Lewis and Clark's figure on the timeline in the year 1804, which was when they departed on the Voyage of Discovery. Look at the other events before, during, and after this year.

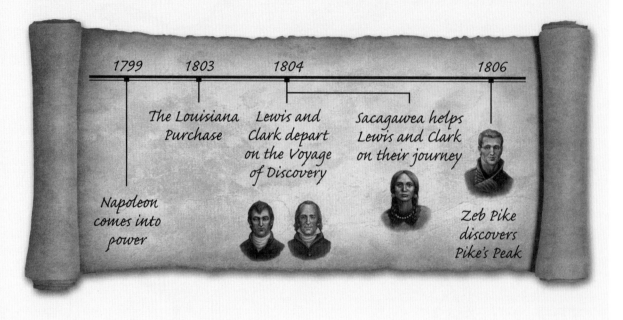

1799   1803   1804   1806

The Louisiana
Purchase

Lewis and
Clark depart
on the Voyage
of Discovery

Sacagawea helps
Lewis and Clark
on their journey

Napoleon
comes into
power

Zeb Pike
discovers
Pike's Peak

Activity

Teamwork was an important part in the success of the Lewis and Clark expedition. Choose a task that you can do with another person such as making something, cleaning something, or doing something. After you complete the task with your partner, talk with your parent about how you could have been more successful.

Wordscramble

Here is a list of scrambled words that relate to the profile you read about Lewis and Clark. Unscramble the letters and write the words correctly.

1. Mwhireeter iseLw _____
2. hoTmsa senorfJfe _____
3. lWialim laCkr _____
4. rpCso fo vDyocesir _____
5. ietxeinpdo _____

6. cciiPfa ecanO _____
7. iooeatrlpxn _____
8. yerastrec _____
9. antipac _____
10. nUedti stetSa _____

True or False

After reading the profile, decide whether each of the following statements about Lewis and Clark is true or false

1. _____ Captain Lewis never actually met President Jefferson.

2. _____ Meriwether Lewis met William Clark while they were both in the navy.

3. _____ Lewis and Clark had great respect for one another.

4. _____ The goal of the Corps of Discovery was to explore the northwestern United States.

5. _____ William Clark was actually first in command of the Corps of Discovery.

Cloze

After reading the profile, try to fill in the blanks with words that make sense about Lewis and Clark. When you are finished, look at the story to find the words that were used in the passage.

The Corps of _____ was hugely successful. They made maps of a part of the country that no one had ever seen before and documented over 300 _____ and _____ for the very first time. Lewis and Clark reached the _____ Ocean; they made it to the far side of America and back. The success of their two-year expedition was largely because they worked so well together. From the very beginning, _____ and _____ shared equal responsibility. And just as they shared responsibilities, they also shared the credit that comes with such an historic _____. Lewis was actually the first in command of the Corps of Discovery, and William Clark was second. Instead of claiming his glory however, Lewis never told the other men. He referred to Clark as "Captain" and no one ever thought differently.

Lewis and Clark Word Search

```
Q O C O R P S O F D I S C O V E R Y Z
V M R I X H E O K F S P X P Z X U S G
B G Z N P E G M L Y U Y C F S P Q T O
T H O M A S J E F F E R S O N L F M N
T P A T C J N I S R F O B I I O V S Q
K S H W I L L I A M C L A R K R Z E C
G R Q M F N B V A H W C P H L A Y C N
F V U K I Z J O X W C A U D Y T P R Z
Y F F E C P N Z Y W F P A P T I H E B
V A Y F O A R M U E A T O B P O G T K
P V F H C E H D F Y P A R A N N S A Z
W S R O E X P E D I T I O N X L M R Q
P G B K A I U C Z Y E N J V I T W Y I
O L I U N I T E D S T A T E S E C Y J
X W M E R I W E T H E R L E W I S H G
```

Word Bank

Meriwether Lewis
Thomas Jefferson
William Clark
Corps of Discovery
expedition

Pacific Ocean
exploration
secretary
captain
United States

Lewis and Clark Crossword

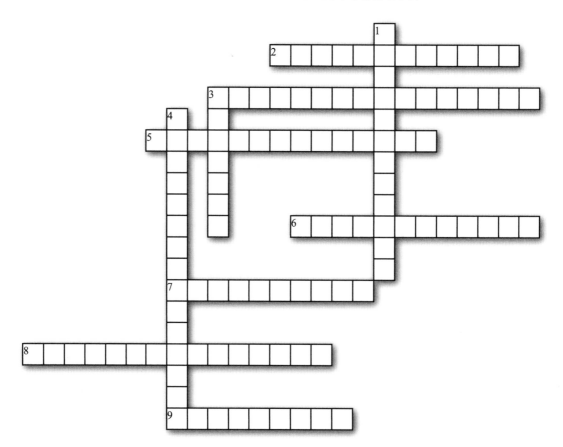

Across

2. Man who was Lewis' commander in the army

3. Group of people sent to explore unknown parts of our country

5. This is something that Lewis and Clark shared equally on their expedition

6. Lewis and Clark were the first men to explore the western part of this country

7. Word that refers to a journey with a purpose; Captain Lewis was asked to lead one

8. Man who became the third president of the United States

9. Before Lewis became leader of the Corps of Discover, he did this job for President Jefferson

Down

1. The destination of the Corps of Discovery

3. This was Meriwether Lewis' rank

4. This man grew up with President Jefferson

Sacagawea

In the year 2000, a new American dollar coin was produced. Congress voted that the new coin would be a symbol of liberty, and that it would picture the Native American woman who helped Lewis and Clark explore the mid-western United States. The woman that you see on the American dollar coin is Sacagawea. It is interesting to note that Congress also voted to include the word "Peace" on the coin. During Lewis and Clark's journey, Sacagawea and her son were symbols of peace to whomever the explorers approached. Men who traveled with women and children were not viewed as a threat to the native tribes they encountered.

Sacagawea was the daughter of a great chief. She had many brothers and sisters, and grew up in a region that is now known as Idaho. When Sacagawea was only ten years old, she was kidnapped by a nearby tribe. They took her to live with them, and she stayed there until the famous expedition of Lewis and Clark began in 1804.

A man named Toussaint Charbonneau married Sacagawea when she was a young girl. Charbonneau was a trapper and hunter who came from Canada. Later, some white men who called themselves the Corps of Discovery came to the village where Sacagawea and her husband lived. They were looking for a trapper and a guide for an extensive journey they were about to begin. Charbonneau asked the men in charge of the expedition, Meriwether Lewis and William Clark, if they would hire him for the job. Not only did they believe that Charbonneau would be very useful, but he mentioned that he had a wife who spoke Shoshone. Lewis and Clark knew that the expedition would be in great need of an interpreter, and so they gratefully accepted Mr. Charbonneau's offer.

The expedition was delayed for about eight weeks when Sacagawea gave birth to her first child. She named her baby Jean-Baptiste, but Sacagawea often called him Pompy, which means firstborn in her native language. Finally, in May of 1804 the Corps of Discovery, along with Toussaint Charbonneau, Sacagawea and her newborn son Pompy, set out on what was to become an historical milestone.

Sacagawea carried Pompy on her back throughout the long and dangerous journey, through rugged and difficult country. The group traveled long distances each day. Not only did Sacagawea have to think about her own safety, but she also had to think of her son's safety. One of the most astonishing factors in Sacagawea's story is that despite many struggles, she never complained. In fact, she kept a cheerful and helpful attitude throughout their travels. This was so amazing to the men she traveled with, that each one who kept a journal commented on it.

A couple of months into the expedition, Sacagawea was riding in a boat that capsized on the Missouri river. Instead of swimming straight to shore, Sacagawea recovered some of the items that had fallen out of the boat. She rescued Lewis and Clark's journals and some of the records they had been keeping. Lewis and Clark wrote some of their most valuable information in those journals, and without them the knowledge we have today about this historical trip would be very different. Lewis and Clark were so pleased with Sacagawea's selfless act that they named a river in her honor.

Sacagawea proved throughout her life that she was very brave. There are few people who could have done such amazing things in such an unselfish way. Lewis and Clark were forever grateful to Sacagawea.

Discussion

1. Why do you think Sacagawea and her son were symbols of peace as the Corps of Discovery traveled into unknown territory?

2. If you could choose five things to take with you on a journey to an unknown and mysterious place, what would they be? Why?

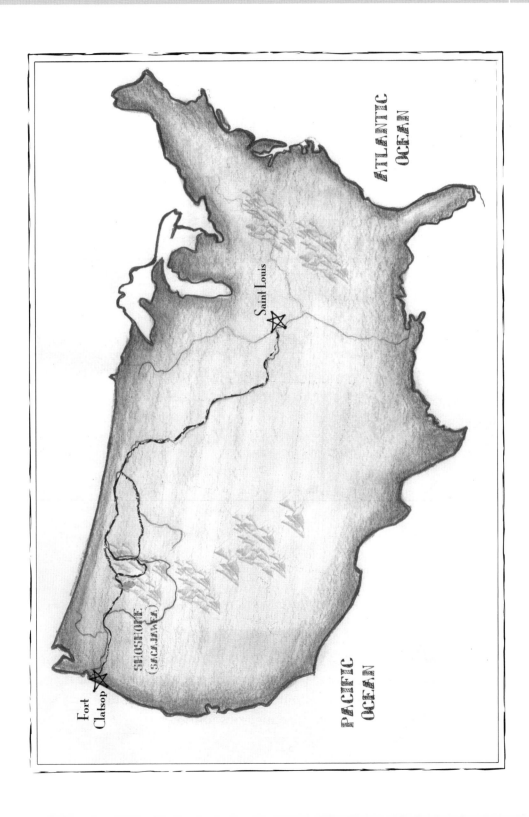

Timeline Review

Put things in perspective. Place Sacajawea's figure on the timeline in the year 1804, which was when she helped Lewis and Clark on their journey. Look at the other events before, during, and after this year.

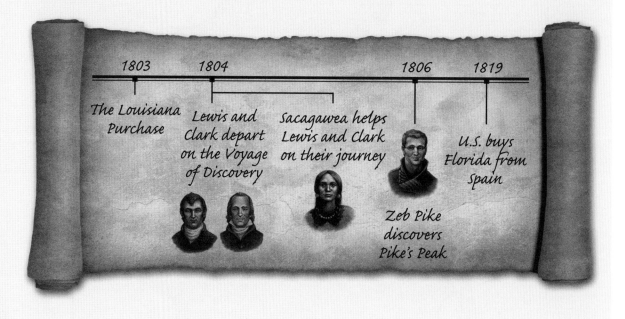

1803 — The Louisiana Purchase

1804 — Lewis and Clark depart on the Voyage of Discovery

Sacagawea helps Lewis and Clark on their journey

1806 — Zeb Pike discovers Pike's Peak

1819 — U.S. buys Florida from Spain

Activity

If you have a backpack, put a five-pound bag of sugar or flour in it. Then wear the backpack all day long – when you're playing, working, and resting. Wear it again the next day, and talk with your parent about what it must have been like for Sacagawea as she carried her baby every day on the dangerous journey.

Wordscramble

Here is a list of scrambled words that relate to the profile you read about Sacagawea. Unscramble the letters and write the words correctly.

1. lodrla _____
2. eplexor _____
3. cpeea _____
4. dIhoa _____
5. soeoSnhh _____
6. irpnteteerr _____
7. opyPm _____
8. feehrucl _____
9. lnujorsa _____
10. lnsehfisu _____

True or False

After reading the profile, decide whether the following statements are true or false:

1. _____ Sacagawea's son, Pompy, was about two years old when they began their journey with the Corps of Discovery.

2. _____ Lewis and Clark wanted Sacagawea and her husband to be cooks on their expedition.

3. _____ Sacagawea and her son were symbols of peace on the journey.

4. _____ Sacagawea carried Pompy on her back.

5. _____ Sacagawea was known for her selfish and gloomy attitude.

Cloze

After reading the profile, try to fill in the blanks with words that make sense about Sacagawea. When you are finished, look at the story to find the words that were used in the passage.

A couple of months into the expedition, Sacagawea was riding in a

_____ that _____ on the Missouri river. Instead of

swimming straight to _____ , Sacagawea recovered some of the items

that had fallen out of the boat. She _____ Lewis and Clark's journals

and some of the _____ they had been keeping. Lewis and Clark wrote

some of their most valuable information in those journals, and without them

the _____ we have today about this historical trip would be very

different. Lewis and Clark were so pleased with Sacagawea's selfless act that they

named a _____ in her honor.

Sacagawea Word Search

```
G X O U G O V Z A H O P L C G O G G Z
K A H W D P S W A S N K F M W P L U J
Z E X P L O R E T U N S E L F I S H E
F S D O L L A R G V T F J K K I B Z C
L I N M G I S Q X B Q Z B E Q N N P T
D P I P O B Z Y S P E A C E A T D N W
F W H Y O I D A H O G C J I J E Z N E
R X A H E Z Z L O B S H N Z L R V I K
F Z Q J J F L A S D S E A K J P J W E
L X P J K F D D H I H E T G Q R H S
F T I L Z Z H F O A G R H N E E U H
P B C F F Q E T N T W F U K Y T G Y E
I V C U X W T Z E Q D U B P E E X O D
T E F Y H J O U R N A L S X K R Y E P
H S X A O C H N D I Q X L B U X S U W
```

Word Bank

dollar

explore

peace

Idaho

Shoshone

interpreter

Pompy

cheerful

journals

unselfish

Sacagawea Crossword

Across

2. When a boat capsized, Sacagawea rescued these important things that belonged to Lewis and Clark

5. To travel around or investigate something or someplace for the first time

6. Name of Sacagawea's tribe

7. What Sacagawea and her son symbolized on Lewis and Clark's journey

10. Place where Sacagawea grew up

Down

1. The job that Sacagawea's husband was hired to do on the expedition

3. There are few people who could have done such amazing things in this way

4. An American coin that has a picture of Sacagawea on it

8. Sacagawea was admired for having this type of attitude

9. The nickname that Sacagawea called her son

Zebulon Pike

S ome people grow up without a vision for their future, and live each day waiting to find a purpose. They're always looking for something that will fill them with hope and motivate their lives. Although some never find that purpose, Zebulon Pike discovered his calling very early in his life. He was born to be an explorer.

Pike's father served under General George Washington during the Revolutionary War, and after the war he stayed in the army. So it was not a surprise when Zeb decided to follow his father and become a military man. He joined his father's regiment, and was soon made a lieutenant. It wasn't long though before he left the army to pursue his true interest, exploration.

When Thomas Jefferson bought the Louisiana Territory in 1803, he purchased the land for 15 million dollars from Napoleon, the Emperor of France. This may seem like a lot of money, but considering the amount of land it was three cents per acre. Even though people during his time thought buying all that land was foolish, President Jefferson wanted the United States to grow and prosper. He saw a bigger picture, and knew that before long the land would be very valuable. For that to happen, President Jefferson needed intelligent, strong, capable men to explore the vast land that he had bought from France. He chose three people to head up that task, Lewis and Clark, and Zebulon Pike. Zeb Pike was sent to explore the southwestern part of our country while Lewis and Clark explored the northwestern region.

Zebulon Pike was a stout, stubborn man, but he was stubborn in a good way. When Zeb was assigned a job, he would do everything he could to get it done. His determination gave him favor with men like Thomas Jefferson. It was largely because of Zebulon's strong will that his expeditions were so successful. Pikes Peak, which Zeb discovered in Colorado, is one of our National Historic Landmarks and is also the most visited mountain in North America.

Some other places named after this great explorer include:

Pikesville, Maryland	Pike County, Ohio
Pike County, Illinois	Pike County, Alabama
Pike County Kentucky	Pike County, Georgia
Pike County, Missouri	Pike County, Indiana
Fort Pike (Louisiana)	Pikes Peak (Iowa)
Pike National Forest (Colorado)	Piketon, Ohio

There is no doubt that Zebulon Pike left quite a legacy, and he is remembered throughout America for his many exploration ventures.

Discussion

1. Stubbornness and determination are very closely related attitudes. People tend to think that determination is better than stubbornness. Can you think of some examples of each attitude? Talk with your parent about what makes them different. Is there anything in your life that you are stubborn about? Is there anything that you are determined about?

2. Locate Pikes Peak on a U.S. map. (Hint: It is in Colorado.) Find information about Pikes Peak at the library or, with your parent's permission, on the Internet. Why is this mountain famous? Tell what you have learned, and then trace or draw the outline of this distinctive peak.

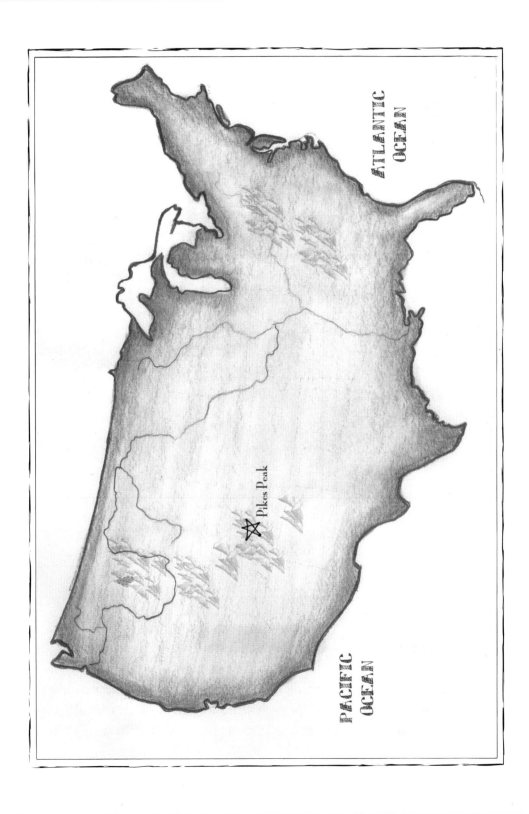

Timeline Review

Put things in perspective. Place Zebulon Pike's figure on the timeline in the year 1806, which was when he discovered Pikes Peak. Look at the other events before, during, and after this year.

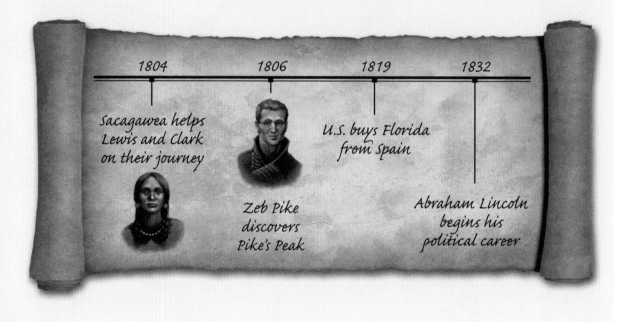

Activity

Use a dictionary to define the words stubbornness and determination. How are the words the same and how are they different? Use a thesaurus to find synonyms and antonyms for each word. Can you think of an animal that would be a good example of each quality? Make an index card for each word and include all the information you found about it. Draw a picture of the animal you chose to illustrate each term.

Wordscramble

Here is a list of scrambled words that relate to the profile you read about Zebulon Pike. Unscramble the letters and write the words correctly.

1. ousprpe _____

2. yarm _____

3. roepxionalt _____

4. oaNpenol _____

5. aeFrnc _____

6. rpeorps _____

7. alpebca _____

8. uwosrtstehne _____

9. ntmeieidnorta _____

10. sscuucfsel _____

True or False

After reading the profile, decide whether the following statements are true or false:

1. _____ Zeb Pike's father was a school teacher.

2. _____ Zeb became a lieutenant in the army.

3. _____ Zeb left the army to follow his true interest, which was farming.

4. _____ President Jefferson chose Zeb to explore the southwestern part of the Louisiana Territory.

5. _____ A mountain in Colorado was named after Zeb.

Cloze

After reading the profile, try to fill in the blanks with words that make sense about Zeb Pike. When you are finished, look at the story to find the words that were used in the passage.

Zebulon Pike was a stout, _____ man, but he was stubborn in a

_____ way. When Zeb was assigned a _____ , he would do

everything he could to get it done. His determination gave him _____

with men like Thomas Jefferson. It was largely because of Zebulon's strong will

that his expeditions were so _____ . Pikes Peak, which Zeb discovered

in _____ , is one of our National Historic Landmarks and is also the

most visited _____ in North America.

Zebulon Pike Word Search

```
Z A R M E R F R A N C E C K Z V T Q Z
W D E T E R M I N A T I O N U N J S L
D C V J Y K V Q V K M P R O S P E R U
N A N V A R M Y K B N N I C P M G J V
A P O S Y J Y S Q I T G D R Q V Y Q H
J A S X K P U R P O S E H B Y I E B Y
V B A W K W I F M S J F G C B N S O G
B L W S V M S L V L Y M L Q J N H I U
D E P Y E X P L O R A T I O N W X I Z
S O U T H W E S T E R N M W W P O T T
A Y G B Z J F G W B A Q Y W A A L F Q
A B N Y X R S Y Q S D J P I J R R Z G
V B G Z I F Z R T S Y W I K F I Y T R
S U C C E S S F U L N M V S F C G W S
D N A P O L E O N C M I B O S F W C C
```

Word Bank

purpose

army

exploration

Napoleon

France

prosper

capable

southwestern

determination

successful

Zebulon Pike Crossword

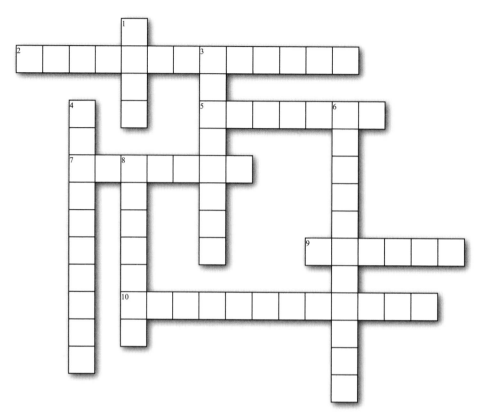

Across

2. Character quality Pike had that is similar to stubbornness

5. President Jefferson wanted the United States to grow and to do this

7. A quality President Jefferson was looking for in the explorers he chose; word that means able to do something well

9. Country that President Jefferson bought the Louisiana Territory from

10. Area of our country that Pike was sent to explore

Down

1. Both Zeb and his father served in this branch of the military

3. The name of the French emperor

4. Zeb's expeditions turned out this way largely because of his strong will

6. What Zebulon Pike's true interest was

8. Some people grow up without a vision and have to wait a long time to find this

Jesse Applegate

On a seemingly average day in the year 1843, three brothers set out on a historic journey that would later be known as the "great migration." They were with a group of 900 people who had all chosen to take the long and treacherous Oregon Trail. Jesse, Lindsay, and Charles gathered their families together, and loaded up all their belongings with the hope of starting a new life. Traveling out west was an opportunity to start fresh, a chance to acquire some land and establish a new home. Jesse Applegate, at the young age of 29, led his wife, their 13 children, and his brothers with their families through the hazardous adventure of the Oregon Trail.

Jesse Applegate would soon discover his great ability to lead. After a dispute over the livestock slowed down the group, the great migration broke into two parties. There was the "light column" and the "cow column." Jesse was captain of the "cow column." The separation had little relevance in the end when the "cow column" was able to stay just a half-day behind the others, with Jesse's direction.

While traveling down the Columbia River, the Applegates had a tragic accident. One of Jesse's sons and his brother Lindsay's son drowned. Their boat capsized, and the boys were lost. It was then that Jesse and Lindsay decided they would establish a safer path for this portion of the trail. The Oregon Trail was a route traveled by many, and they knew that more tragedies like theirs could occur, and did. In fact, many lives had been lost on this perilous trail. It was time to make a change.

Jesse and Lindsay set out to find a safer path for those traveling to Oregon while their brother Charles Applegate took care of the families. The Applegate brothers were accompanied by a group of about ten other men. Their goal was to find and clear a functional trail that avoided the Columbia River. Through their determination and strength, the expedition was a success. They discovered a southern route that is known as the Applegate Trail, or the South Road. This new route was shorter and safer than the Oregon Trail. It was still a difficult journey to take on, but the new trail was a change for the better. The Applegate Trail was used for many years, by many families, as an alternative to the Oregon Trail. Today it is recognized as a National Historic Trail.

Jesse Applegate was always working towards a cause. While living in Oregon he was a member of the legislative committee, and represented his county at the Oregon Constitutional Convention. He was the primary author of the document that declared Oregon a territory of the United States. Then, in 1860 Jesse used his influence to sway Oregon's vote to Republican. His efforts assisted in the election of one of America's greatest presidents, Abraham Lincoln.

Jesse Applegate built a home in Oregon where he lived until his death at the age of 77. He named it Yoncalla after a local Indian tribe. Late in his life, because of the wisdom he had gained over many years, Jesse was known as the "Sage of Yoncalla." Jesse Applegate fought hard for whatever he believed in. He lived an influential life that benefited all those around him, and he left a trail of bravery, sacrifice, and leadership through the history of Oregon.

Discussion

1. Have you ever tried to find an easier or better way to do something? How did it turn out? If you haven't, can you think of anything that you would like to find a better way to do?

2. Talk with your parent about shortcuts he or she might use when driving from one place to another. Is the shortest way always the best way? Why or why not?

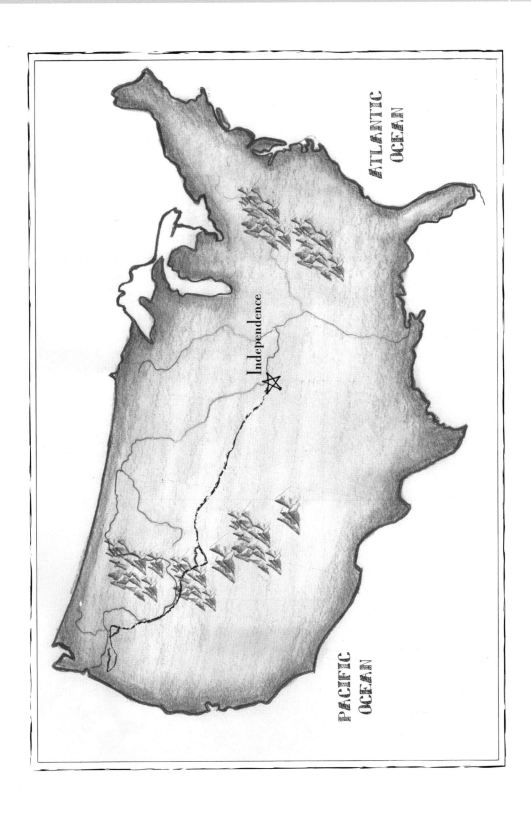

Timeline Review

Put things in perspective. Place Jesse Applegate's figure on the timeline in the year 1846, which was when he blazed the Applegate Trail. Look at the other events before, during and after this year.

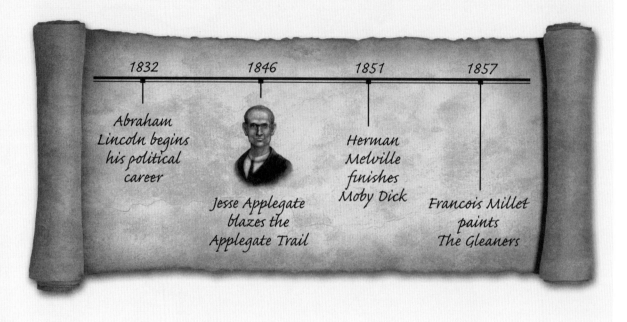

| 1832 | 1846 | 1851 | 1857 |

Abraham Lincoln begins his political career

Jesse Applegate blazes the Applegate Trail

Herman Melville finishes Moby Dick

Francois Millet paints The Gleaners

Activity

Much like the Pilgrims, settlers going west left everything they knew behind. Make a list of things you would take with you to remind you of home. Now look at your list, choose the three most important things to you, and tell why.

Wordscramble

Here is a list of scrambled words that relate to the profile you read about Jesse Applegate. Unscramble the letters and write the words correctly.

1. rgeta aioinmtrg _____

2. Oreong rTial _____

3. srzohuaad _____

4. bitlayi _____

5. ccdeanit _____

6. hecnag _____

7. nhuotS dRao _____

8. raltainevet _____

9. hautro _____

10. olacalnY _____

True or False

After reading the profile, decide whether the following statements are true or false:

1. _____ Jesse and his brothers traveled by themselves to Oregon.

2. _____ The Oregon Trail was considered a safe way to travel to the northwest.

3. _____ The Applegate family suffered a terrible tragedy on their trip.

4. _____ Jesse and Lindsey discovered a path that was shorter and safer than the Oregon Trail.

5. _____ Jesse always fought hard for things he believed in.

Cloze

After reading the profile, try to fill in the blanks with words that make sense about Jesse Applegate. When you are finished, look at the story to find the words that were used in the passage.

Jesse and Lindsay set out to find a _____ path for those traveling to

Oregon while their brother Charles Applegate took care of the families. The

Applegate brothers were accompanied by a group of about _____ other

men. Their _____ was to find and clear a functional trail that avoided

the Columbia _____. Through their determination and strength,

the expedition was a _____. They discovered a _____ route

that is known as the Applegate Trail, or the South Road. This new route was

_____ and safer than the Oregon Trail. It was still a _____

journey to take on, but the new trail was a change for the better. The Applegate

Trail was used for many years, by many families, as an alternative to the Oregon

Trail. Today it is recognized as a National Historic Trail.

Jesse Applegate Word Search

```
B Y U E T A B B C T W T Y J A N L X U
B D A O B R T G K Y L G V G L T Y X Z
R K J R I Y A Q C C H L I O T K O G G
G O J E F R U J V H A J X M E E N S X
R Y W G T P T N K A Z D M Q R B C O T
U N P O A F H X C N A F W Q N W A U X
P A V N P A O G W G R E V F A J L T J
S B Z T I C R V J E D G T G T C L H A
B I P R G C O D S U O I W Q I B A R O
X L Z A G I C M R D U C D L V X V O E
P I A I D D Y Z K W S K M R E M K A G
F T B L N E C G G X A U S O D O Y D Y
D Y W H R N S Z A S M A M U P R P N C
X G R E A T M I G R A T I O N J S N D
L Y C V S U N H F O K Z S F T A A L G
```

Word Bank

great migration   change
Oregon Trail   South Road
hazardous   alternative
ability   author
accident   Yoncalla

Jesse Applegate Crossword

Across

4. A person who writes something
5. The name of the southern route that the Applegate brothers discovered
7. After their tragic loss, the Applegate brothers decided it was time for this
8. Another word for skill; "leading" was one of these for Jesse
9. Another word for "substitute" or "instead of"

Down

1. The journey that the Applegate brothers set out on came to be known by this name
2. Another word for dangerous; used in Profile to describe the Oregon Trail
3. Name of an Indian tribe that lived near Jesse's home
4. While on the Columbia River, the Applegates suffered one of these
6. The long, treacherous path that people followed into the west

Francois Millet

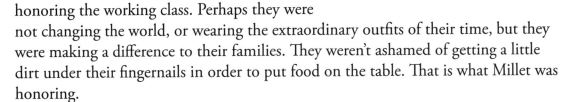

Francois Millet wanted to be different, and he wanted to make a difference. He was a painter who lived during a time when most paintings were extremely dramatic, portraying only disastrous events or great heroism. Francois Millet chose to portray the beauty of simplicity. He revealed the lives of peasants, or poor farmers, to the world in a new light. For example, in his painting *The Gleaners*, Millet shows us a portrait of three women who are gleaning after a harvest. A common practice for peasants, gleaning is picking up what the harvesters have left behind. Peasants had never been the subject of a painting like this before. Through it, Millet was honoring the working class. Perhaps they were not changing the world, or wearing the extraordinary outfits of their time, but they were making a difference to their families. They weren't ashamed of getting a little dirt under their fingernails in order to put food on the table. That is what Millet was honoring.

Francois Millet was born to a family of peasant farmers, and he bravely chose to illustrate the various life tasks of the working class. His paintings came from firsthand knowledge because he grew up with the realities of peasant life. No doubt he overcame many obstacles to achieve success. Millet was 20 years old when he left his home in Normandy, France, to go to Paris. He had received a scholarship to study painting there, and so began his renowned career. Some people were displeased with his suspected political views. Others admired his vision. Among his admirers was a painter whose name would soon be engraved in history, Vincent van Gogh.

Millet was one of the leading influencers who started an art school called the Barbizon School. At this school painters of a new era drew together. They decided that, like Millet, they wanted to be different from the other artists of their time. These painters were considered a part of the "naturalism" movement. This was a movement in which nature was the focus. Many painters in this movement chose to simply portray nature's magnificence through landscapes. Millet however, put people in his paintings. These people were by nature average and plain, but somehow within the golden light and soft colors used by Millet, they became exquisite.

In 1859, when Francois Millet was 45, he painted *The Angelus.* This would become one of his most famous paintings. In *The Angelus,* there are two farmers in plain clothes standing with bowed heads. They were painted in the same angelic, golden hue as *The Gleaners.* They stand with a field of crops behind them, and the hazy figure of a church in the distance. The man in the painting holds his hat in his hands, and the woman's hands are clasped tightly together. Both seem humble and somber. The name of the painting, *The Angelus,* is taken from a Catholic prayer time that occurs three times a day: morning, noon, and evening. In Millet's painting one can assume that the farmers heard the bell from the far away church and stopped their work to pray. Perhaps they are praying for a good harvest, perhaps they are thanking God for what they have – no one knows. What can be seen is that this painting portrays these farmers in a stunning light.

Francois Millet was a revolutionary. His paintings did not change the fact that peasants continued to live in poverty and difficulty. But perhaps because of Millet they held their heads a little higher than before.

Discussion

1. Before Millet's time, most artists painted things that were grand and dramatic. Millet went against that practice and painted things that were simple. Do you think his paintings made simple things seem more grand? Think about what you learned about Shakespeare's life and work. How are Millet and Shakespeare alike?

2. Naturalism is a movement in art that focuses on nature. There are many people who feel that paintings or photographs of nature are beautiful art. Do you agree? What places or things in nature would you consider beautiful or dramatic art? Think of a beautiful painting or photograph of nature that you have seen and describe it.

Wordscramble

Here is a list of scrambled words that relate to the profile you read about Francois Millet. Unscramble the letters and write the words correctly.

1. limitycips _____

2. anpsesat _____

3. Nmdanyro _____

4. Pasri _____

5. lngeesra _____

6. artmulnsia _____

7. aacpndlsse _____

8. gelAnsu _____

9. naiingpt _____

10. avsterh _____

Timeline Review

Put things in perspective. Place Francois Millet's figure on the timeline in the year 1857, which was when he painted *The Gleaners*. Look at the other events before, during, and after this year.

1851 — Herman Melville finishes Moby Dick

1857 — Francois Millet paints The Gleaners

1861-1865 — The U.S. Civil War

1869 — War and Peace by Leo Tolstoy is published

1884 — France gives the Statue of Liberty to the United States

Activity

Look at a painting by Francois Millet at the library or, with your parent's permission, on the Internet. What do you notice about the painting's colors? What do you notice about the people in the pictures? When you look at his paintings, can you tell how Millet felt about his subjects?

Cloze

After reading the profile, try to fill in the blanks with words that make sense about Francois Millet. When you are finished, look at the story to find the words that were used in the passage.

Francois Millet wanted to be different and to make a _____. He lived during a time when most paintings were extremely dramatic, portraying only disastrous events or heroism in its fullest capacity. _____ chose to portray the _____ of _____ He revealed the lives of _____, or poor farmers, to the world in a new light. For example, in his painting *The Gleaners*, Millet shows us a portrait of three women who are _____ after a harvest. A common practice for peasants, gleaning is picking up what the harvesters have left behind. Peasants had never been the subject of a _____ like this before. Through it, Millet was _____ the working class. Perhaps they were not changing the world, or wearing the beautiful outfits of their time, but they were making a difference to their families. They weren't ashamed of getting a little dirt under their fingernails in order to put food on the table. That is what Millet was honoring.

Sequencing

Number the following events from Francois Millet's life in the order they were introduced in his profile. Use the numbers 1–5.

A. _____ He left home to go to art school in Paris.

B. _____ Millet painted "The Angelus."

C. _____ Francois Millet was born to a family of peasant farmers.

D. _____ Millet helped start a movement in art that focused on nature.

E. _____ Vincent van Gogh admired his work.

Francois Millet Word Search

```
O T N O Y I Q C F U Y O L L Z T I R Y
Y X O N D Y J T L F W P O F Y O S A B
P A R I S K S M A U R A I L C Z I T A
K D M U R O T T N Q U I D Z U D M Y J
H B A L H F C G D I W N T M J C P D K
I Z N H A R V E S T Y T M A C I L G S
D C D E M N A M C B P I X W N X I W M
I F Y N D O Q F A I B N T A I Z C I Z
K Y N G B Q X Z P P N G H D K D I B X
G J C P Y C B U E W X J K H H J T S O
N P E A S A N T S B I J Q G U C Y L E
Z Z N Z U F A N G E L U S G H K U Q Z
A U L U U S W B R G L E A N E R S S I
R Z S U N A T U R A L I S M H B O Q Y
E E G M K V I W Y D Z O J Q C M A A T
```

Word Bank

simplicity

peasants

Normandy

Paris

Gleaners

naturalism

landscapes

Angelus

painting

harvest

Francois Millet Crossword

Across

3. Francois Millet wanted to show the beauty of this
4. A painting of two farmers with bowed heads
5. Place where Millet moved to study painting
7. Name of an art movement in which nature was the focus
9. Another word for poor farmers
10. Place in France where Francois grew up

Down

1. A painting of three women picking up what harvesters have left behind
2. Many painters showed nature's magnificence through this type of painting
6. A type of art that involves color
8. The gathering of crops when they are ripe

Timeline

1232

The earliest
known rockets
are used

1275

Marco Polo
enters the
service of Kublai
Khan

1200

1429

Joan of Arc
is appointed
military
commander

1440

1492

Columbus
Discovers
America

Leonardo da Vinci
completes painting
The Last Supper

1400

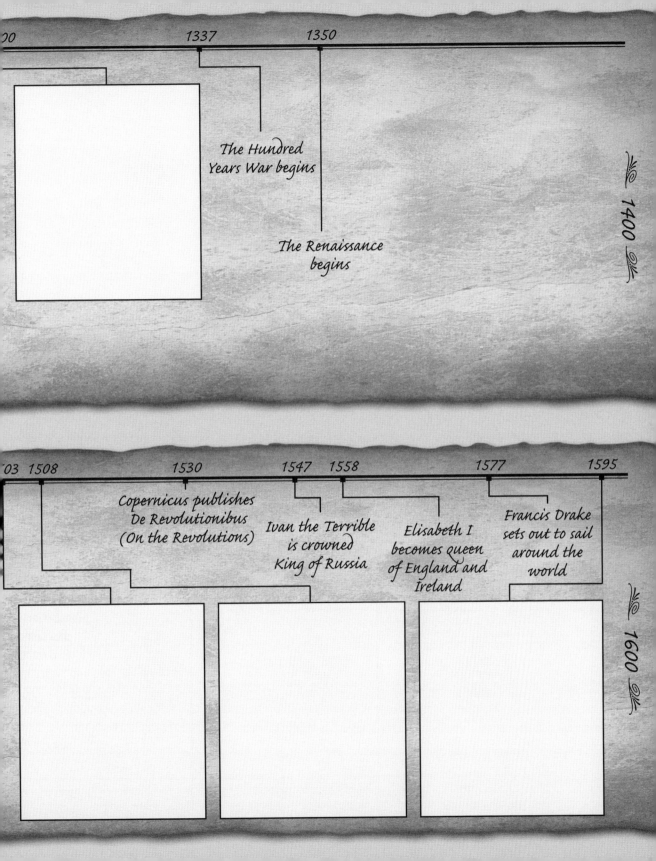

1337   1350

The Hundred
Years War begins

The Renaissance
begins

1400

03 1508   1530   1547 1558   1577   1595

Copernicus publishes
De Revolutionibus
(On the Revolutions)

Ivan the Terrible
is crowned
King of Russia

Elisabeth I
becomes queen
of England and
Ireland

Francis Drake
sets out to sail
around the
world

1600

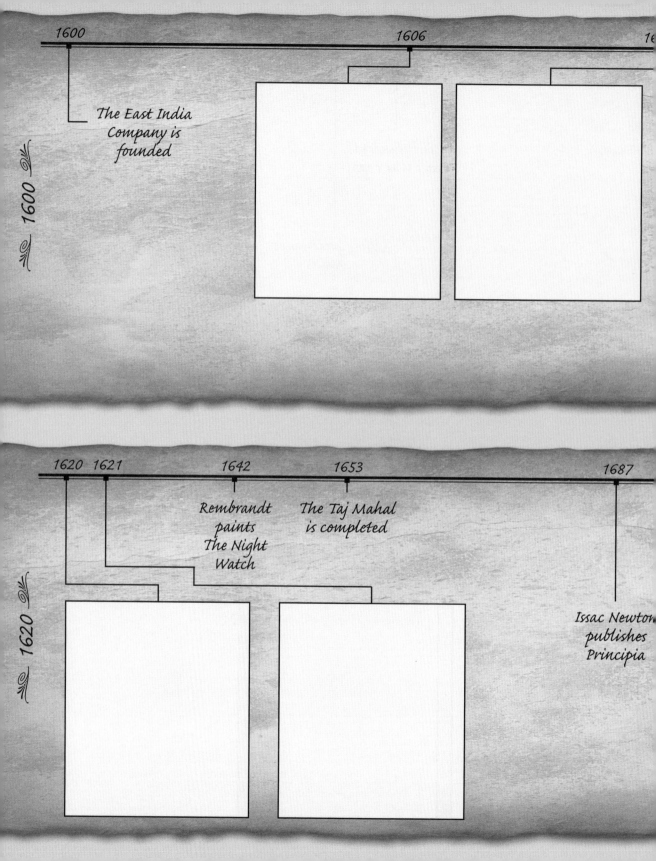

1600 1606 16

The East India
Company is
founded

1600

1600

1620 1621 1642 1653 1687

Rembrandt
paints
The Night
Watch

The Taj Mahal
is completed

Issac Newton
publishes
Principia

1620

1620

1616

1709

1721

1732

1742

1753

1768

1620

Bartolomeo
Cristofori makes
the first Piano

Bach composes
the Brandenburg
concertos

The Liberty Bell, hung in the
Pennsylvania State House,
cracks with the first stroke of
the clapper

1770

1774   1776

Ben Franklin returns to America to help with the Revolutionary War

1770

1803   1804

The Louisiana Purchase

1800

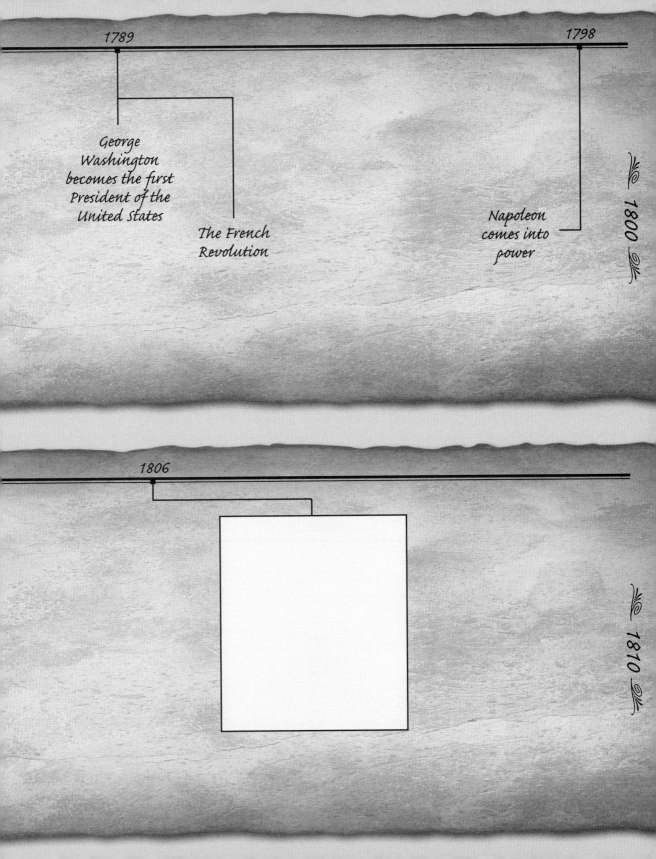

1789

1798

George
Washington
becomes the first
President of the
United States

The French
Revolution

Napoleon
comes into
power

1800

1806

1810

1810

1819
U.S. buys
Florida from
Spain

1832
Abraham
Lincoln begins
his political
career

1846

| 1851 | 1857 | 1861-1865 | 1869 | 1884 |

Herman
Melville
finishes
Moby Dick

The U.S.
Civil War

France gives the
Statue of Liberty
to the United
States

War and Peace
by Leo Tolstoy is
published

1890

Marco Polo
The Travels of Marco Polo c. 1300

Johannes Gutenberg
Designs printing press 1440

Leonardo da Vinci
Begins painting *Mona Lisa* 1503

Michelangelo
Paints the Sistine Chapel 1508

William Shakespeare
Writes *Romeo and Juliet* 1595

John Smith
Sails to Jamestown 1606

Galileo
Publishes his beliefs 1610

Pocahontas
Travels to England 1616

William Bradford
Sets sail for the New World 1620

Squanto
Helps the Pilgrims 1621

Benjamin Franklin
Poor Richard's Almanack 1732

George Frideric Handel
Messiah first performed 1742

James Cook
First trip around the world 1768

Thomas Jefferson
Declaration of Independence 1776

Mozart
Begins piano concertos 1776

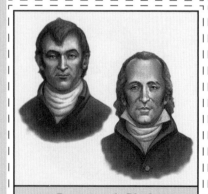

Lewis and Clark
Set out to explore the West 1804

Sacagawea
Helps Lewis and Clark 1804

Zebulon Pike
Discovers Pikes Peak 1806

Jesse Applegate
Blazes the Applegate Trail 1846

Francois Millet
Paints *The Gleaners* 1857

Answer Key

Marco Polo

Wordscramble:

1. explorer
2. journey
3. adventure
4. Cathay
5. Kublai Khan
6. captain
7. book
8. mapmakers
9. dreams
10. faraway

Cloze:

seeing
China
watched
learn
families
people
places
things

True/ False:

1. F
2. F
3. T
4. T
5. T

Johannes Gutenberg

Wordscramble:

1. books
2. reading
3. poetry
4. printing press
5. invention
6. letters
7. affordable
8. paper
9. knowledge
10. library

Cloze:

machine
stories
poems
hand
rare
wealthy
money
ordinary

Sequencing:

A. 3
B. 1
C. 4
D. 2

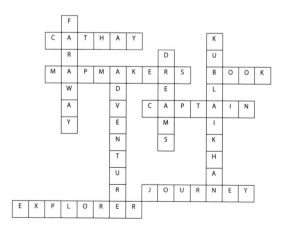

Leonardo da Vinci

Wordscramble:

1. inventor
2. artist
3. scientist
4. thinking
5. creativity
6. painting
7. distracted
8. Mona Lisa
9. museum
10. admire

Cloze:

ability
portrait
years
famous
emotion
common
expression
secret

True/ False:

1. T
2. F
3. T
4. T
5. F

Michelangelo

Wordscramble:

1. art
2. symbols
3. destiny
4. talent
5. sculpture
6. Sistine Chapel
7. scaffold
8. drawing
9. painting
10. ceiling

Cloze:

unhappy
sculpting
greatest
loved
design
drawing
life
character

True/ False:

1. F
2. T
3. F
4. F
5. T

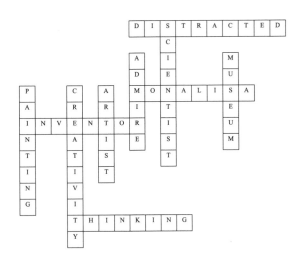

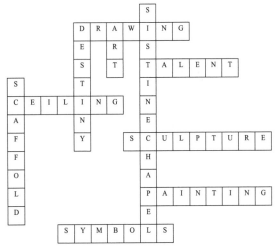

William Shakespeare

Wordscramble:	Cloze:	True/ False:
1. Stratford	plays	1. F
2. England	sonnets	2. F
3. comedies	poems	3. T
4. histories	Shakespeare	4. F
5. tragedies	humor	5. T
6. author	comedies	
7. plays	histories	
8. sonnets	tragedies	
9. William		
10. Theatre		

John Smith

Wordscramble:	Cloze:	Sequencing:
1. journeys	leadership	A. 3
2. soldier	Chief Powhatan	B. 4
3. hero	respected	C. 1
4. Jamestown	burned	D. 2
5. colony	treatment	E. 5
6. unpopular	left	
7. leader	England	
8. nobility	Jamestown	
9. survive		
10. Virginia		

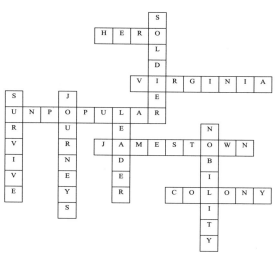

Galileo

Wordscramble:	Cloze:	True/ False:
1. scientist	telescope	1. F
2. trial	heavens	2. T
3. treason	smooth	3. T
4. universe	appearance	4. F
5. Aristotle	revolves	5. T
6. telescope	theory	
7. craters	center	
8. observations	thanks	
9. Newton		
10. Beliefs		

Pocahontas

Wordscramble:	Cloze:	Sequencing:
1. Powhatan	visit	A. 4
2. playful	food	B. 1
3. colony	governor	C. 5
4. helping	strange	D. 2
5. ambush	crown	E. 3
6. warning	bow down	
7. prisoner	upset	
8. ransom	trade	
9. John Rolfe		
10. Princess		

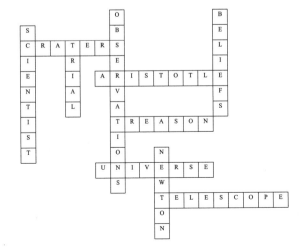

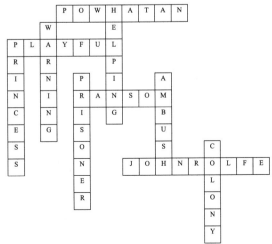

William Bradford

Wordscramble:	Cloze:	True/ False:
1. Mayflower	give up	1. T
2. refuge	stood	2. F
3. Pilgrims	strong	3. F
4. purpose	brave	4. F
5. Separatists	hardships	5. T
6. noble	leader	
7. believers	voice	
8. governor	decision	
9. leadership		
10. service		

Squanto

Wordscramble:	Cloze:	Sequencing:
1. Tisquantum	peace	A. 2
2. character	crops	B. 1
3. Patuxet	fertilize	C. 4
4. adventure	catch	D. 3
5. journey	interpreter	E. 5
6. slaves	guide	
7. monks	respect	
8. smallpox	God	
9. interpreter		
10. peace		

Benjamin Franklin

Wordscramble:	Cloze:	Sequencing:
1. famous	contributions	A. 5
2. scientist	control	B. 4
3. inventor	eight	C. 1
4. patent	mission	D. 2
5. lightning	help	E. 3
6. library	respected	
7. newspaper	colonies	
8. leadership	hope	
9. letters		
10. France		

George Frideric Handel

Wordscramble:	Cloze:	True/ False:
1. Handel	London	1. T
2. Messiah	Handel	2. F
3. Bach	Messiah	3. T
4. harpsichord	Easter	4. T
5. masterpiece	composer	5. F
6. inspiration	Westminster	
7. Hallelujah Chorus	Beethoven	
8. King George	greatest	
9. coronation		
10. composer		

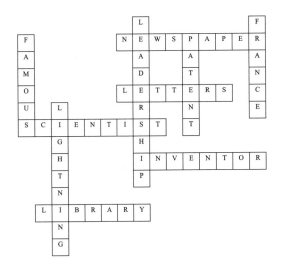

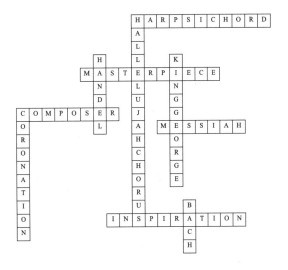

James Cook

Wordscramble:

1. navigation
2. astronomy
3. mapping
4. Antarctic
5. Australia
6. Captain Cook
7. scurvy
8. Master
9. Commander
10. Navy

Cloze:

recognition
surveying
explore
England
person
explore
superior
discovered
farther
Antaractic

Pacific
Newfoundland
European
coastline
Hawaiian

Sequencing:

A. 2
B. 3
C. 1
D. 4
E. 5

```
R I S C U R V Y T R N U E G X C P Q T
Q F V A U W G W B X S L C V L C H E U
C O M M A N D E R D X Y M P F A H N B
G P A N T A R C T I C J M L V P F A F
O E S L C Y B K A A U U N D E T Q V H
A C T L F V J A U S T R A L I A T Y L
N P E A D F Q C R T Y U V R Y I D U P
J Q R E G P A M I R A N I T Y N B V M
Z K X L X O R S Y O V L G R H C Q U G
J E L P K R P T Q N T Q A G U O O S H
K L X X Q R I E V O X W T Y H O H I C
J P M A P P I N G M S G I Z Q K W N S
B J L X U Z I T N Y H P O L O R V W V
O P D J K Z B S N S N N N Z V E Q X W
N T R F H O R W N F U F U X V K M J E
```

Thomas Jefferson

Wordscramble:

1. mission
2. author
3. wisdom
4. governor
5. representative
6. president
7. troubled
8. inspiring
9. humility
10. Monticello

Cloze:

third
responsibilities
speech
talents
leadership
two
popular
people

Sequencing:

A. 5
B. 2
C. 3
D. 1
E. 4

```
M W C R U G G S C C M M E D W G G O X
E M S M D A U T H O R I O H U O S O C
I A B T I P G G U F P S F M Z I T A H
G O V E R N O R M R U S J E Q E R N C
J O E E W U Q L I O T I I T G J O F X
D E Q V X Q P W L Z W O W U Q S U J Y
B W O L W D F R I Z G N V U S W B X G
L I I F B M O N T I C E L L O J L P L
N S D J O B O H Y W H R S J T D E H U
V D O Y C E I N S P I R I N G W D O V
K O O Y V Q X P R E S I D E N T V G X
K M C E R E P R E S E N T A T I V E C
B B K A I I D Y J A V A D H M G Z V M
A W N N O E N N U L Y Y B E R K D I R
V B Y N Y B F R N D G A B B T T I H V
```

Mozart

Wordscramble:	Cloze:	Sequencing:
1. Leopold	father	A. 5
2. piano	composers	B. 1
3. Mozart	concerts	C. 2
4. concerts	Bach	D. 4
5. Salzburg	Mozart	E. 3
6. violin	Salzburg	
7. talent	violin concertos	
8. musician	legacy	
9. composer		
10. Vienna		

Lewis and Clark

Wordscramble:	Cloze:	True/ False:
1. Meriwether Lewis	Discovery	1. F
2. Thomas Jefferson	Maps	2. F
3. William Clark	plants	3. T
4. Corps of Discovery	animals	4. T
5. expedition	Pacific	5. F
6. Pacific Ocean	Lewis	
7. exploration	Clark	
8. secretary	expedition	
9. captain		
10. United States		

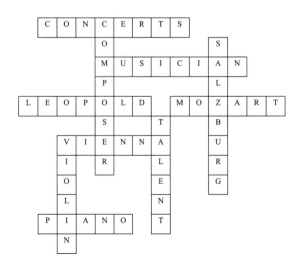

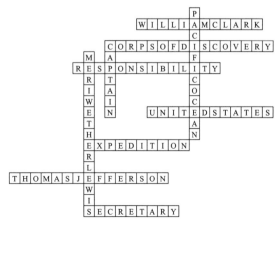

Sacagawea

Wordscramble:	Cloze:	True/ False:
1. dollar	boat	1. F
2. explore	capsized	2. F
3. peace	shore	3. T
4. Idaho	rescued	4. T
5. Shoshone	records	5. F
6. interpreter	knowledge	
7. Pompy	trip	
8. cheerful	river	
9. journals		
10. unselfish		

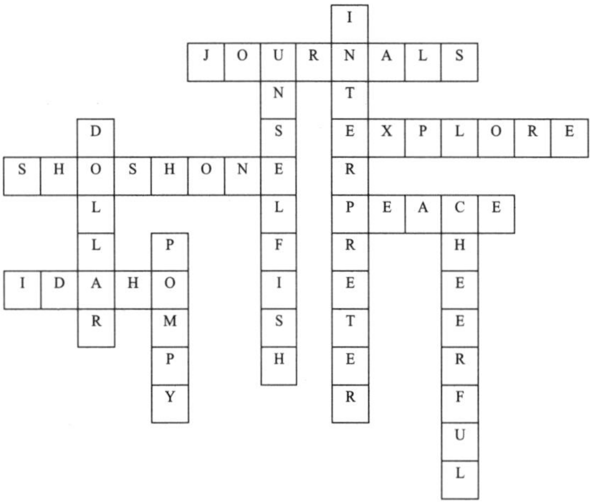

Zebulon Pike

Wordscramble:	Cloze:	True/ False:
1. purpose	stubborn	1. F
2. army	good	2. T
3. exploration	job	3. F
4. Napoleon	favor	4. T
5. France	will	5. T
6. prosper	successful	
7. capable	Colorado	
8. southwestern	mountain	
9. determination		
10. successful		

Sacagawea word search:

```
G X O U G O V Z A H O P L C G O G G Z
K A H W D P S W A S N K F M W P L U J
Z E X P L O R E T U N S E L F I S H E
F S D O L L A R G V T F J K K I B Z C
L I N M G I S Q X B Q Z B E Q N N P T
D P I P O B Z Y S P E A C E A T D N W
F W H Y O I D A H O G C J I J E Z N E
R X A H E Z Z L O B S H N Z L R V I K
F Z Q J J F L A S D S E A K J P J W E
L X P J K F D D H I H E T G Q R J H S
F T I L Z Z H F O A G R H N E E J U H
P B C F F Q E T N T W F U K Y T G Y E
I V C U X W T Z E Q D U B P E E X O D
T E F Y H J O U R N A L S X K R Y E P
H S X A O C H N D I Q X L B U X S U W
```

Zebulon Pike word search:

```
Z A R M E R F R A N C E C K Z V T Q Z
W D E T E R M I N A T I O N U N J S L
D C V J Y K V Q V K M P R O S P E R U
N A N V A R M Y K B N N I C P M G J V
A P O S Y J Y S Q I T G D R Q V Y Q H
J A S X K P U R P O S E H B Y I E B Y
V B A W K W I F M S J F G C B N S O G
B L W S V M S L V L Y M L Q J N H I U
D E P Y E X P L O R A T I O N W X I Z
S O U T H W E S T E R N M W W P O T T
A Y G B Z J F G W B A Q Y W A A L F Q
A B N Y X R S Y Q S D J P I J R R Z G
V B G Z I F Z R T S Y W I K F I Y T R
S U C C E S S F U L N M V S F C G W S
D N A P O L E O N C M I B O S F W C C
```

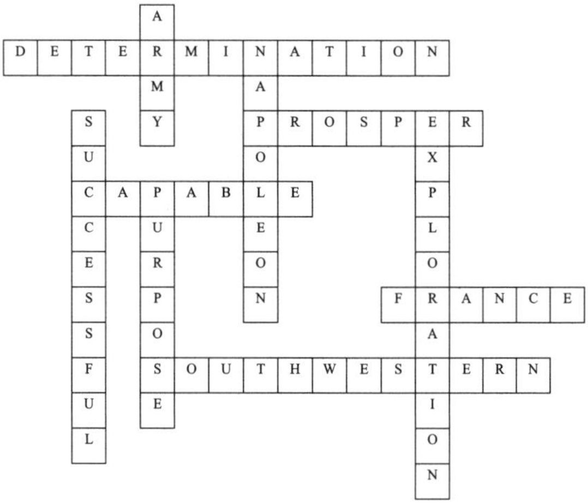

(Two crossword puzzle grids appear at the bottom of the page.)

Jesse Applegate

Wordscramble:	Cloze:	True/ False:
1. great migration	safer	1. F
2. Oregon Trail	ten	2. F
3. hazardous	goal	3. T
4. ability	River	4. T
5. accident	success	5. T
6. change	southern	
7. South Road	shorter	
8. alternative	difficult	
9. author		
10. Yoncalla		

Francois Millet

Wordscramble:	Cloze:	Sequencing:
1. simplicity	difference	A. 2
2. peasants	Francois Millet	B. 5
3. Normandy	beauty	C. 1
4. Paris	simplicity	D. 4
5. gleaners	peasants	E. 3
6. naturalism	gleaning	
7. landscapes	painting	
8. Angelus	honoring	
9. painting		
10. harvest		

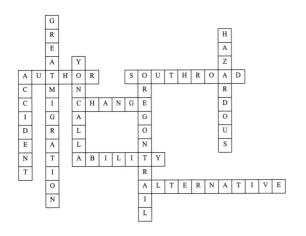

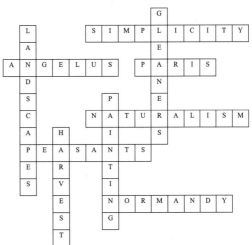

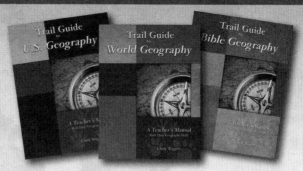

Trail Guide to Geography Series -
by Cindy Wiggers

Three books in the *Trail Guide to ...Geography* series include U.S., World, and Bible geography. Each book provides clear directions and assignment choices to encourage self-directed learning as students create their own personal geography notebooks. Daily atlas drills, mapping activities, and various weekly assignment choices address learning styles in a way that has kids asking for more! Use each book over several years by choosing more difficult activities as students grow older.

Trail Guide features:
• Weekly lesson plans – for 36 weeks
• 5-minute daily atlas drills (2 questions/day, four days/week)
• 3 levels of difficulty – all ages participate together
• Weekly mapping assignments
• A variety of weekly research and hands-on activity choices

Student Notebooks are available on CD-ROM

Trail Guide Levels
The *Trail Guide* Levels are just a guide. Select a level according to student ability, and match level with the appropriate atlas or student notebook.

• Primary: grades 2–4
• Intermediate: grades 5–7
• Secondary: grades 8–12
All 3 levels in each book!

Note: Primary is ideal for independent 4th graders. Second and third graders will need plenty of guidance. If your oldest is 2nd–3rd grade range, please consider *Galloping the Globe* or *Cantering the Country* first.

Trail Guide to U.S. Geography
Grades 2 - 12

"The *Trail Guide to U.S. Geography* provides lots of guidance while allowing for (and encouraging) flexibility and this is just the balance most homeschool moms need! The manual is easy to navigate and I am very impressed with how thoroughly material is covered. This resource is destined to be a favorite with homeschool families for years to come!"
–Cindy Prechtel, homeschoolingfromtheheart.com
Paperback, 144 pages, $18.95

Trail Guide to World Geography
Grades 2 - 12

"We have the *Trail Guide to World Geography* and **love** it!! We are using it again this year just for the questions... I will never sell this guide!! I am looking forward to doing the U.S. one next year."
–Shannon, OK
Paperback, 128 pages, $18.95

Trail Guide to Bible Geography
Grades 2 - 12

"Here is another winner from Geography Matters! *Trail Guide to Bible Geography* is multi-faceted, user-friendly, and suited to a wide range of ages and abilities."
–Jean Hall, Eclectic Homeschool Association
Paperback, 128 pages, $18.95

Galloping the Globe
Grades K - 4
by Loreé Pettit and Dari Mullins

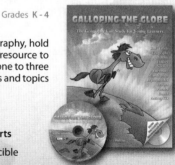

"If you've got kindergarten through fourth grade students, and are looking for unit study material for geography, hold on to your hat and get ready for *Galloping the Globe!* Loreé Pettit and Dari Mullins have written this great resource to introduce children to the continents and some of their countries. This book is designed to be completed in one to three years, depending on how much time you spend on each topic. And for each continent, there are suggestions and topics galore." –Leslie Wyatt, www.homeschoolenrichment.com

Organized by continent, incorporates student notebooking, and covers these topics:
• Basic Geography   • History & Biographies   • Literature   • Science
• Bible   • Activities   • Internet Sources   • Language Arts

This new 2010 edition of *Galloping the Globe* includes an Activity CD-ROM jam-packed with all the reproducible activity sheets found in the book plus added bonus pages. Paperback with CD-ROM, 272 pages, $29.95

Cantering the Country
Grades 1 - 5
by Loreé Pettit and Dari Mullins

Saddle up your horses and strap on your thinking caps. Learning geography is an adventure. From the authors who brought you *Galloping the Globe,* you'll love its U.S. counterpart, *Cantering the Country.* This unit study teaches a wide range of academic and spiritual disciplines using the geography of the U.S. as a starting point. With this course, you won't have to put aside one subject to make time for another. They're all connected! This comprehensive unit study takes up to three years to complete and includes all subjects except math and spelling. Incorporates student notebooking and covers these topics:

• U.S. Geography   • Character   • Science   • Language Arts
• Activities   • Literature   • Civics   • History & Biographies & More

In addition to the 250+ page book, you will receive a CD-ROM packed full of reproducible outline maps and activities. Dust off your atlas and get ready to explore America! Paperback with CD-ROM, 272 pages, $29.95

The Ultimate Geography and Timeline Guide

by Maggie Hogan and Cindy Wiggers

Grades K - 12

Learn how to construct timelines, establish student notebooks, teach geography through literature, and integrate science with activities on volcanoes, archaeology, and other subjects. Use the complete multi-level geography course for middle and high school students. Now includes CD-ROM of all reproducible activity and planning pages. Use for all students kindergarden through high school. Paperback with CD-ROM, 353 pages, $39.95

- 18 Reproducible Outline Maps
- Teaching Tips
- Planning Charts
- Over 150 Reproducible Pages
- Over 300 Timeline Figures
- Lesson Plans
- Scope and Sequence
- Flash Cards
- Games

Mark-It Timeline of History

There's hardly no better way to keep history in perspective than creating a timeline in tandem with your history studies. This poster is just the tool to do so. Write or draw images of events as they are studied, or attach timeline figures to aid student understanding and comprehension of the topic at hand. 23" x 34". Laminated, $10.95, Paper (folded), $5.95

Adventures of Munford Series

by Jamie Aramini

Although he's just two parts hydrogen and one part oxygen, Munford is all adventure. He can be rain, snow, sleet, or steam. He has traveled the world in search of excitement. Throughout history, he has been present at some of the most important and world-changing events. Fun and educational, Munford will inspire your children to learn more about many of history's greatest events. These readers make a great addition to your learning experience in areas such as history, geography, and science. This book series was written on an elementary reading level, but provides plenty of read-aloud entertainment for the entire family! Paperback, $8.95.

The American Revolution

In this adventure, Munford travels to colonial America and experiences first hand the events leading to the American Revolution. He meets famed American Founding Fathers, such as Samuel Adams, Thomas Jefferson, and George Washington. He joins the Sons of Liberty under cover of night to dump tea into Boston Harbor. He tags along for Paul Revere's most famous ride, and even becomes a part of the Declaration of Independence in a way that you might not expect!

The Klondike Gold Rush

In this adventure, Munford finds himself slap into the middle of the Klondike Gold Rush. He catches gold fever on this dangerous, yet thrilling, adventure. Meet some of the Gold Rush's most famous characters, like gold baron Alex McDonald or the tricky villain named Soapy Smith. Take a ride on the Whitehorse Rapids, and help Munford as he pans for gold. This is an adventure you won't soon forget!

Munford Meets Lewis & Clark

Join Munford on an epic adventure with Meriwether Lewis and William Clark, as they make their perilous journey in search of the Northwest Passage to the Pacific Ocean.

Munford Meets Robert Fulton

Join Munford— the world's most daring water molecule in his latest adventure! Munford joins forces with inventor Robert Fulton, inventor of the world's first practical steam boat!

Eat Your Way Through the USA

by Loreé Pettit

Taste your way around the U.S.A. without leaving your own dining room table! Each state has its unique geographical features, culinary specialities, and agricultural products. These influence both the ingredients that go into a recipe and the way food is prepared. Compliment your geography lesson and tantalize your tastebuds at the same time with this outstanding cookbook.

This cookbook includes a full meal of easy to follow recipes from each state. Recipes are easy to follow. Though they aren't written at a child's level, it's easy to include your students in the preparation of these dishes. Cooking together provides life skills and is a source of bonding and pride. More than just a cookbook, it is a taste buds-on approach to geography. Spiral bound, 118 pages, $14.95

Eat Your Way Around the World

by Jamie Aramini

Get out the sombrero for your Mexican fiesta! Chinese egg rolls... corn pancakes from Venezuela...fried plantains from Nigeria. All this, and more, is yours when you take your family on a whirlwind tour of over thirty countries in this unique international cookbook. Includes a full meal of recipes from each country. Recipes are easy to follow, and ingredients are readily available. Jam-packed with delicious dinners, divine drinks, and delectable desserts, this book is sure to please.

The entire family will be fascinated with tidbits of culture provided for each country including: Etiquette hints, Food Profiles, and Culture a la Carté. For more zest, add an activity and violà, create a memorable learning experience that will last for years to come. Some activities include: Food Journal, Passport, and World Travel Night. Spiral bound, 120 pages, $14.95

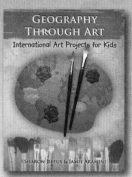

Geography Through Art
by Sharon Jeffus and Jamie Aramini

Geography Through Art is the ultimate book of international art projects. Join your children on an artistic journey to more than twenty-five countries spanning six continents (includes over a dozen United States projects). Previously published by Visual Manna as *Teaching Geography Through Art*, Geography Matters has added a number of enhancements and practical changes to this fascinating art book. Use this book as an exciting way to supplement any study of geography, history, or social studies. You'll find yourself reaching for this indispensable guide again and again to delight and engage students in learning about geography through the culture and art of peoples around the world. Paperback, 190 pages, $19.95

Lewis & Clark - Hands On
Art and English Activities
by Sharon Jeffus

Follow the experiences of Meriwether Lewis and William Clark with hands on art and writing projects associated with journal entries made during the Corps of Discovery Expedition. Ideal for adding interest to any Lewis and Clark study or to teach drawing and journaling. Includes profiles of American artists, step by step drawing instructions, actual journal entries, and background information about this famous adventure. Paperback, 80 pages, $12.95

Profiles from History - Volume 2
by Ashley (Strayer) Wiggers

Profiles from History - Volume 2 is a book filled with the heroes of our country's past. In it you will discover twenty men and women that greatly contributed to the formation and building of America. The strongest connection we can have to history is a human connection. This book will enable you to get to know the characters in a unique way, and find out just what it was that made them heroes of America's growth and freedom. Paperback, $16.95

Also availible:
Profiles from History - Volume 1. Paperback, $16.95   *Profiles from History - Volume 3.* Paperback, $16.95

- Reproducible Outline Maps -

Reproducible outline maps have a myriad of uses in the home, school, and office. Uncle Josh's quality digital maps provide opportunities for creative learning at all ages. His maps feature rivers and grid lines where possible, and countries are shown in context with their surroundings. (No map of Germany "floating" in the center of the page, here!) When students use outline maps and see the places they are studying in context they gain a deeper understanding of the subject at hand.

Uncle Josh's Outline Map Book

Take advantage of those spontaneous teaching moments when you have this set of outline maps handy. They are:

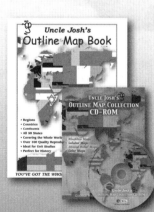

- Over 100 reproducible maps
- 15 world regions
- Continents with and without borders

- 25 countries
- Each of the 50 United States
- 8 U.S. regions

Useful for all grades and topics, this is by far one of the best book of reproducible outline maps you'll find. Paperback, 128 pages, $19.95

Uncle Josh's Outline Map Collection CD-ROM

In addition to all maps in *Uncle Josh's Outline Map Book* the CD-Rom includes color, shaded-relief, and labeled maps. Over 260 printable maps plus bonus activities. CD-ROM (Mac & Windows), $26.95

- Large-scale Maps -

Large-scale maps are great for detail labeling and for family or classroom use. Laminated Mark-It maps can be reused for a variety of lessons. Quality digital map art is used for each of the fifteen map titles published and laminated by Geography Matters. Choose from large scale continents, regions, United States, and world maps. US and World available in both outline version and with state, country, and capitals labeled. Ask about our ever expanding library of full, color shaded-relief maps. Paper and laminated, each title available separately or in discounted sets.

TRAIL GUIDE TO LEARNING

Introducing… ***The Trail Guide to Learning series***, an innovative new curriculum from Geography Matters. This series provides all the guidance and materials necessary to teach your children the way you've always wanted—effectively, efficiently, and enjoyably. But most of all, *Trail Guide to Learning* equips you to achieve the foremost objective of a homeschooling program—developing and nurturing relationships with your children! The tutoring approach makes each lesson individual, yet flexible enough to meet the needs of several grades at once. The sourcebook provides the instruction, clearly laid out in daily sections that make lesson planning a breeze. Just add in the necessary resources for success, available in our money-saving packages, and you'll have a curriculum for multiple grade levels that will last all year and cover every subject but math!

Paths of Exploration
Grades 3-5

Paths of Settlement
Grades 4-6

Paths of Exploration takes students on a journey. Follow the steps of famous explorers and pioneers across America and let geography be your guide to science, history, language skills, and the arts. This journey will teach students HOW to think by asking, answering, and investigating questions about our great country's beginning and growth. The paths of the explorers are seen through multidisciplinary eyes, but always with the same goals: to make learning enjoyable, memorable, and motivating. This full one-year course for 3rd, 4th and 5th graders (adaptable for 2nd and 6th) covers six units in two volumes.

Walk the *Paths of Settlement* with famous Americans such as George Washington, Patrick Henry, John and Abigail Adams, Francis Scott Key, Clara Barton, Robert E. Lee, Abraham Lincoln, Laura Ingalls Wilder and Booker T. Washington. They built upon the trail blazed by brave explorers and their actions teach us the principles of freedom and citizenship founding and expanding our country, strengthening us in times of war and binding us together in times of struggle.

Your children will take a tour of America, yesterday and today, learning about geography, geology, and weather along the way! Multimedia makes music and history come to life, while literature, art and activities beautifully illustrate the times. Language skills are included equipping your children to express their thoughts and reflect their learning naturally.

Paths of Progress
Grades 5-7

Look online now for more information and to view sample pages.

www.TrailGuidetoLearning.com • **800-426-4650**

About the Author

Ashley (Strayer) Wiggers grew up in the early days of the home schooling movement taught by parents, Greg and Debbie Strayer, who are authors of numerous home schooling materials. A home school graduate, Ashley enjoyed a 10-year career as a national champion synchronized swimmer and is currently the Public Relations Director at Geography Matters. Ashley speaks at home school seminars across the country, edits a monthly online newsletter for Geography Matters, and is the author of the *Profiles from History* series.

Ashley makes her home in Somerset, KY, with her husband, Alex, and can't wait to someday continue the home school philosophies and ideals that her parents and in-laws have passed on with her own children.